I'm too

for my
Volvo

I'm too

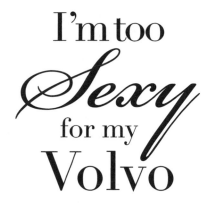

Sexy

for my

Volvo

A Mom's Guide
to Staying *Fabulous*

Betty Londergan

adams media
avon, massachusetts

Published by
Adams Media, an F+W Publications Company
57 Littlefield Street, Avon, MA 02322. U.S.A.
www.adamsmedia.com

ISBN: 1-59337-502-6

Printed in the United States of America.

J I H G F E D C B

Library of Congress Cataloging-in-Publication Data
Londergan, Betty.
I'm too sexy for my Volvo : a mom's guide to staying fabulous /
by Betty Londergan.
p.   cm.
ISBN 1-59337-502-6
1. Mothers—Life skills guides. 2. Postnatal care—Life skills guides.
3. Mothers—Health and hygiene—Popular works. I. Title.

HQ759.L575 2006
649'.10242--dc22

2005034594

This publication is designed to provide accurate and authoritative information with regard to the subject matter covered. It is sold with the understanding that the publisher is not engaged in rendering legal, accounting, or other professional advice. If legal advice or other expert assistance is required, the services of a competent professional person should be sought.
—From a *Declaration of Principles* jointly adopted by a Committee of the American Bar Association and a Committee of Publishers and Associations

Many of the designations used by manufacturers and sellers to distinguish their product are claimed as trademarks. Where those designations appear in this book and Adams Media was aware of a trademark claim, the designations have been printed with initial capital letters.

Interior illustrations by Frank Rivera.

This book is available at quantity discounts for bulk purchases.
For information, please call 1-800-872-5627.

"If you can't be a good example,
you'll just have to serve
as a horrible warning."

—Catherine Aird

dedication

This book is for Lulu,
who made me a mother.

For Larry,
who gave me my sense of humor back.

And for my dad,
who always said, "Good things happen."

The Journey

Acknowledgments

In the spirit of acknowledgment (or spreading the blame), I must first recognize Sarah Tomley, for giving me the idea for this book and refusing to let me off the hook in writing it, and my editor, Kate Epstein, who whipped the whole thing into shape. I would also like to thank my early readers for being such enthusiastic and gentle critics: Mimi Kaupe, Judith Hain, Laurie Dibeler, Rita Marshall, Ginger O'Neill, Dana Kleiman, Joy Goldstein, Michelle Botelho, Kathy Martin, and Richard Graglia; my mother-in-law Rhoda and sister-in-law Alyce for their constant support; my sisters Susan, Kathy, Mary Lou, and Bonnie and their reading girls: Carolynn, Amy, Marie, Christy, and Donna; and finally, the formidably talented and inspiring art directors who helped me visualize the book (and sell the bloody thing): Abby Chase, Pat Carlin, Liz Meitus, and Graig Silverman.

A special note of recognition to the super-fabulous Amy Berkower of Writer's House for first taking this on and having such faith in me; to Jodi Reamer, who always laughed at my jokes; and finally to my agent, Daniel Lazar, who is tireless, relentless, hilarious, and amazing. Thank you with all my heart.

Introduction

this is not your mother's pregnancy book

Well, at least it's not *my* mother's pregnancy book. For one thing, my mother didn't need a pregnancy book because she was young, had her master's degree in physiology, and was fertile as the Tigris and Euphrates valley. My dad popped in a seed, she swelled up like a grape (annoyingly retaining her cute figure), and out popped one of the eight of us.

Alas, the helter-skelter trajectory of my romantic life didn't exactly follow the straight-arrow path of my mother's. And once I did (temporarily) settle down in matrimonial bliss, I found I had inadvertently taken up residence on the wrong side of the motherhood tracks. After three years of infertility counseling in which the only diagnosis the doctors could come up with was "hostile cervical mucus," I was pushing thirty-seven and praying for a baby, with the kind of witless desperation of a wino praying to win the lottery.

Then I hit the pregnancy jackpot. And boy, did I need serious help.

I'm Too Sexy for My Volvo is the book I could never find but would have clasped to my (for once) substantial bosom like a new best friend. The kind of book that would tell you to buy great bracelets because when the baby finally shows up, you're going to have 7,000 photos of your forearms. A book that could give an honest appraisal of what it feels like to be nine months pregnant. (Think of the Hindenburg, seconds before attack.) A book that prepares a mother for the greatest, most challenging, and all-consuming love affair of her life, while still admonishing her not to throw the Blahniks out with the bathwater. That's what *I'm Too Sexy for My Volvo* is all about—an alternative baby book for new and experienced mothers alike. Let's get to it.

So, you're pregnant.

Congratulations!!!

Not only will you look unspeakably hideous for the next nine months, you can also kiss your life, as you know it, a fond and final farewell. The good news is that you'll also lose your heart to the Precious Bundle, but let's face it, your life and your figure are a pretty hefty price to pay for that privilege. Nevertheless, you've made your bed and now you've got to sleep in it. (Of course, if you'd slept in it a little more and schtupped in it a little less, you wouldn't be in this state of bliss.)

Never mind. From here on out, everything is about The Baby.

Wait a minute! Rewind. Rethink. Reassess that.

From now on, everything is about the baby—*except* for that shallow and lovely part of you that still wants to look pretty and have nice things and enjoy a little peace and quiet, and read and lie around in baths admiring your navel, if you can still see it. The part of you that's never going to be content to be a decorous old matron when clearly, you're a highly fabulous, kick-ass babe with places to go and men to do. (Oops!) That's the endangered part of motherhood I'm talking about here—and let me assure you, it's a facet that's been sadly, badly neglected and may, in fact, be on the verge of complete extinction. No kidding. About 75 million pounds of social pressure is about to descend on you, demanding that you not only completely forfeit your life, your independence, and your sacred selfish shallowness to motherhood, but that you smile while you sign the papers.

Respectfully, I'd like to interject this gentle suggestion: "Get a grip, sweetheart." The First Rule you need to learn is that, much as you adore your kid, it is every bit as important to Be Adorable. And that's not just because if you're a cute mom, you'll produce cute kids. No, cuteness is and always should be an end in itself. Not something you achieve for your kids or husband or random construction workers.

Listen up, mama. There is literally no limit to the life your kids will want you to give up—so you'd better draw the line in the sand now. Resolve not to throw in the towel on things that make you feel deliciously alive, simply because you're throwing in the wash about forty times a day. It is possible to resist the relentless pressure to be selfless, and *I'm Too Sexy for My*

Volvo seeks to illuminate that path. This book is all about how to keep sane, shameless, and shallow while you're being a caring, sharing mom. And if I can help just one mother crawl out of the ooze of total self-denial back into the relative paradise of sporadic self-indulgence, I'll consider that my time on the planet has been well spent. (Well, that and a couple million dollars, palatial homes, and an unending supply of awe-inspiring wine, but I digress . . . .)

A brief caveat: *I'm Too Sexy for My Volvo* is not exclusively for stay-at-home moms or working moms, older moms or teenage moms, ex-prom-queen moms or computer geek moms, single moms or nuclear moms. If you didn't get the memo, let me be the first to break it to you: *All* moms get put through the grinder. This book is an equal opportunity rant about the importance of being frivolous while you're busy raising the planet's next generation. There are at least a hundred thousand books out there on motherhood that will scare you silly, lest you not measure up. My motto is: Lighten up! Anybody can be a great mom. It takes creativity, courage, and commitment to be a shallow, fabulous mom. With no further ado, here are The Mother Rules.

important disclaimer

No rules in this book should be construed as the least bit scientific or medically sound. In fact, a good bit of it has been grossly exaggerated for humorous purposes. In advertising we call this kind of thing "anecdotal," so we don't get sued. Just so you know.

. . . and another thing

Because I'm such a strident, opinionated gasbag, I decided to let a few of my women friends share their Rules in this book. Just to give a second opinion, as it were. But they have to be set off somehow because this is, after all, my book. So when you see the speaking bubble, you'll know it's not my shallow voice you're hearing.

CHAPTER ONE

Pregnancy Rules:
The First 3 Months

a small inkling

I loved my first months of pregnancy. I felt like I had a delicious secret. I was still (relatively) slim. And now I had an excuse for eating virtually nonstop. Things were perfect! Okay, maybe not quite 100 percent perfect, since I was not married to the father of my baby, nor did wedding bells seem to be in the cards for me and my Mr. Wrong. But other than that minor setback, I felt almost ridiculously lucky. I had a great job in advertising, and because I was a partner in the firm, there was technically nobody in a position to call me on the carpet if someone walked in and found me zonked out on it, drooling into the fake-Persian pattern. I also had a ferociously loyal cadre of women friends who fell into formation around me like a flying wedge, thus diverting me from the terrifying view of what I was winging directly into: life as a single mother. Finally, I dropped into pregnancy like a piglet takes to mud—with total

1

enthusiasm and a natural gift for wallowing. I felt in the pink of health, never missed a meal, and pranced around feeling incredibly proud of myself for finally getting knocked up.

However your first trimester unspools—whether you're sick or not, worried or not, packing on the pounds or not—this is still a time when you need to take care of yourself. Your whole success as a mother depends on how you act right now! (Just kidding. You've got plenty of time and will have thousands of opportunities to screw up and/or redeem yourself, believe me.) By taking care of yourself, I don't mean reading the nutrition charts for the 4,000th time. Of course you're going to do that. What desperately requires focus now is that lovely wild and free spirit inside that is about to fade into the woodwork unless you pay her a little attention.

May I suggest a baker's dozen (yum!) of early pregnancy regimens?

RULE #1:
Take pictures of yourself. Naked.
Seriously, you may think you're not even showing and you may even think you look ridiculous, but trust me, you will treasure the sight of those tiny little bumps and swells when your Precious Bundle is a snotty fifteen-year-old. Or a wailing two-year-old. It is a miracle to grow a person inside you, and you want to document it. So even if you can't stand the sight of yourself, shove those pictures into a safe place and remember where you shoved them because I guarantee you, you're

going to get all weepy over them in about ten years. (You also won't believe how young and cute you looked and will wonder why you were ever so hard on yourself.)

Trust me on this. I can't find my Playmom photos and I'm heartbroken about it.

RULE #2:
Shake, rattle, and roll.

Quick, before you can't waddle around the floor anymore, grab your mate (or your best friend), get out there, and shake your moneymaker. Actually, you don't even need a partner, nor do you have to make the effort to two-step out the front door. Just throw on some baggy pants, crank up your CD

great cds to dance to

Abba's Greatest Hits
Buena Vista Social Club
Saturday Night Fever
Soundtrack to Boogie Nights
*Diana Ross & The Supremes: The Ultimate
    Collection*
Gwen Stefani's *Love, Angel, Music, Baby*
Aretha Franklin's *Greatest Hits*
Nellyville
Soul 2 Soul's *Keep on Movin'*
Deep Forest
Al Green's Greatest Hits

player, and bop around your kitchen or across your living room floor.

If you're feeling self-conscious, take Ellen DeGeneres as your role model. She's boogie-down proof that it's almost impossible to dance and be depressed at the same time. Moving to the music will make you feel great, it's good exercise, and it's excellent for the baby. In fact, an introduction to really loud music in utero has been scientifically proven to improve future napping. (Not really, I totally made that up, but it sounds as though it could be true.) Plus, you'll need to get your moves down for those nights when the baby won't sleep and the only thing that gets those little eyes closing is the sound of Nelly rapping and the familiar feeling of you swooping across the floor. Go to it.

RULE #3:
Buy nice soaps.

A couple of years ago, I gave my friend Mimi two enormous bars of fragrant verbena soap as a hostess gift and to this day, she thinks that I am the sheer epitome of soapy self-pampering. I don't have the heart to tell her I'm far too cheap to actually buy those soaps for daily use myself. But when I was pregnant, I splurged all the time, and so should you. For at least these nine months, when you're bound to be spending lots of time in the tub admiring your strange and wonderful body, treat yourself like your own special houseguest. Lay your hands on some handcrafted verbena or lavender soap—the very best you can find. Choose subtle scents that aren't going to make you gag later on. Your sense of smell during pregnancy is like a hog's during truffle season—almost appallingly keen—so do yourself a favor and make your bathroom a gentle, fragrant, and embracing place. It can make a world of difference in your day. Slap down the six bucks a bar and lather up.

Looking for a fabulous resource for handmade, lusciously decadent, yet somehow reasonably priced soaps? Try Copa Soaps in my own beloved Philadelphia (*www.copasoaps.com*).

supporting evidence from dana's school of economics

Okay, so before you got pregnant, you probably spent about $30 a week on wine and/or cocktails at groovy bars and restaurants. (Or in my case, $60.) At $6 a glass, for five glasses of wine, you duly received about five to six hours of wine enjoyment.

But now that you're With Child, you're not drinking, so that $30 goes back into your Discretionary Income column. Now, if you spend $30 of that Discretionary Income on five lovely bars of soap, at about thirty showers and baths from each bar, you will realize a grand total of more than fifty hours of bathroom bliss (at a conservative twenty minutes per bathing incident).

If you're anything like me, you'd choose the five hours of wine-induced happiness over the fifty hours of good clean fun without a second's hesitation. But you're pregnant. So you might as well take that Unspent Discretionary Income and sink it into a soap investment that's out there stimulating the global economy. In nine months, you can go back to stimulating all of Napa.

RULE #4:

**Have lots of sex if you feel like it—
or roll over if you don't.**

Why is it that women whose pregnancies bring out the Lusty Ho' inside always seem to want to share those instincts with women who just want to snooze through the nine months and be left alone? Beats me. Personally, I felt incredibly revved up when I was pregnant—but I totally support a woman's right to choose *The New Yorker* over a roll in the hay any day of the week. Of course, if there is some mind- and spine-bending sexual advice to dish out here, I'm probably not the one to be serving it up. I've never been a big proponent of the candle-light striptease and peekaboo lingerie (much to my husband's sorrow), and all that effort seems even more absurd when your see-through teddy is the size of Shaq's jersey. My advice is simply to follow your instincts and don't stress over sex. Remember, your libido never lies. (Most husbands will hate this advice, but I'm standing by it.)

RULE #5:

Worry not.

It took me so long to get pregnant, and I was so sure it would never happen, that when it finally did, I was sure it couldn't last. I worried constantly. I looked for signs of miscarriage so frequently, people thought I had a terrible bladder infection. In fact, I was enmeshed in an incessant internal dialogue that went something like this:

Okay, it's all going to be fine because the doctor said he can see the heart beating and that's a super good sign so why don't we just try to relax here . . . Oh right, as if God is going to let somebody like me have a baby, not after all the funky things I've done, especially with Oscar back in college . . . Wow, he was so completely hot, I can't believe he had that other wife and baby . . . Not to mention all the mortal sins I've committed . . . Oh, so now we're going back to fourth-grade Catholic school? Why not get out the crown of thorns while we're at it? . . . This is ridiculous, I have got to start thinking positive here . . . Just take deep, cleansing breaths, that's better, I'm feeling whole and peaceful and calmly pregnant . . . But what if something goes wrong? I don't think I can stand it because now I've really, really got my heart set on this baby . . . Wait a minute! Didn't I have about three cosmopolitans that night two weeks ago before I knew I was pregnant? That could totally cause brain damage. Oh no, I think I'm cramping, Oh please don't let it be that! I promise I will never ever lie or cheat or curse or think bad thoughts about anybody, just please please please please let me have this baby . . . Okay, God, I'm just going to the bathroom to check one more time, so please remember our deal, okay?

Allowing yourself to worry and obsess about all the things that might go wrong is dumb, not to mention a waste of time, and a lame excuse for self-indulgence. If you're going to indulge yourself in something, for godsakes, head for the Ben & Jerry's counter for a big, honking waffle cone. Wallowing in worry won't deflect a single event from happening in the future, can't change anything that happened in the past, and serves only to ruin the present—while giving you saggy, baggy jowls. (Or maybe it was all that Cherry Garcia?) Whatever. Resolve not to worry.

Once I hit the magic three-month safety mark, I gave myself permission not to worry one single bit more, and assiduously lived up to that. Happiness followed. Just like the Bobby McFerrin song said.

RULE #6:X
Mum's the word.

Just because you're not worrying doesn't mean it's time to start blabbing. Resist the temptation to tell anybody your little secret until you cruise safely past the magical twelve-week mark. If someone does ask, don't tell. Zip it. Put a sock in it. Press the mute button. Why? Because if, God forbid, something bad does happen, you won't have the added horror of dozens of people you hardly know walking up and asking when your due date is. Granted, it won't make you feel better if no one knows, but it also won't make you feel a hundred times worse. And if you commit to not telling a single soul, that probably means you'll only tell a dozen or so of your very closest friends, whose support you will absolutely require if something does go wrong. If you are so wound up and atwitter that you don't know what to do with yourself, focus on choosing an OB. That should keep you busy for a couple of months.

abbie's open book policy

The minute I found out I was pregnant, I went out and told everybody I knew. Close friends and family. Strangers in line at the grocery store. Random commuters on the train. I found a way to work my big news into all kinds of conversations, non sequiturs be damned. "Sure is cold today." "Sure is, and **since I'm pregnant,** I think I feel the cold even more!" "Are you in the express lane with all those items?" "Yes, but **since I'm pregnant,** I'm technically shopping for two!" What's the big deal about waiting to tell people? If it doesn't work out, I'll still be heartbroken and want to talk about it, not deny it ever happened. And if I keep it a secret for three months, I'll miss ninety days of being able to talk about it, brag about it, and bore people to death with my big news. No way. I'm coming out with it.

RULE #7:
Choose Dr. Right.
Selecting an obstetrician can be a daunting challenge. For one thing, with malpractice insurance premiums skyrocketing, fewer and fewer OBs are practicing (although it might help if they'd stop describing it as "practicing"). The choice can seem so momentous, and you're likely to have so little concept of what you're in for, that it's easy to become paralyzed with uncertainty. Then there's the all-too-frequent case of the buttinsky

friends and family who are desperate to make the decision for you because they have the perfect doctor and the ideal method of delivery and the only hospital anyone in their right mind would ever consider. Hang tough, honey pie. This is *your* baby and you should have it any way and any place you want.

I've even heard that some shallow people choose their doctor based on the hotel quality of the hospital where the doctor delivers. Can you imagine? Yeah, me too! Hey, if you're not having a problematic pregnancy, why shouldn't you have sheets with impressively high thread counts as well as gobs of attention from the nurses? (Not to mention that fancy champagne dinner which, believe me, only sounds good now and will look about as appealing as lawn clippings when you've just gone through eighty-five hours of labor.)

Of course, the obstetrician selection is complicated by the distinct possibility that you'll go through a rigorous decision-making process now, and still end up looking at an entirely new face between your legs come delivery time, because OBs generally share birthing duties with the other docs in their office. The father of my baby had a personal relationship with my OB, so Dr. Reid sweetly agreed to personally deliver our Precious Bundle. That sealed the deal for me, and Dr. Reid did indeed turn out to be Dr. Right.

If you don't have someone with connections to suggest an OB, get a recommendation from a veteran mother who's on your same wavelength. (The wavelength caveat is important. If a woman is nothing like you, why assume that you'd choose the same person to cozy up to your uterus?) In the initial interview, you'll probably be able to tell if you want to go through the next nine months with the doctor by the vibe of the office, the nurses (big factor), and by the amount of time you're accorded to ask questions and feel comfortable. (The annoying long wait is always a given.) This might also be a great time to explore a few midwifery and/or doula practices nearby, in case you decide to go that route. (See Rule #42 for more on that good idea.)

RULE #8:

Write it out.

When the urge to run out and shop becomes overwhelming (pretty much my response to crisis, confusion, boredom, and joy), do not head for a maternity shop. You'll only buy stuff that is going to be about four sizes too small when your body expands beyond anything you've ever imagined possible. Instead, go to a bookstore and buy yourself some beautiful journals and nice pens so you can record what you're thinking and feeling. Pregnancy is a time of great introspection and a lovely thing to capture and reflect upon once labor is safely behind you. A journal will also provide a superb place to vent about all the pressures of your life—which will prove vastly entertaining to look back upon when the Precious Bundle arrives and you come to understand what the term "time-challenged" truly means. While you're in the bookstore, you will no doubt be tempted to buy a few of the thousand baby books that promise to reveal the true path of motherhood. Avoid the ones that make it sound too complicated, too cutesy, or too predictable. Likewise, avoid the books that make it sound too scary. Now's the time to bolster your self-confidence, not blast it out of the water. Browse wisely, letting your intuition be your guide. (But by all means, do splurge and buy ten copies of *I'm Too Sexy for My Volvo* for all your friends.)

RULE #9:
Sisterhood is powerful.

The great huge clique of motherhood just got a new member: you! This is big news. Now you'll get to talk with authority about scintillating topics like cloth versus disposable, breast versus formula, vaginal versus sections. Yes, being pregnant links you with every other mother on the planet, and that can be simultaneously a little claustrophobic and immensely comforting. At the very least, it will give you a never-ending focus of conversation with your mother-in-law or your Cruella De Vil boss-lady, both of whom absolutely *have* to be nice to you now.

Draw closer to all your women friends. Start a book club with your favorite females. Make a point of going out to dinner with the girls. Take a Saturday morning weekly walk with a woman you want to get to know. In all likelihood, your mate is not going to be able to satisfy your desire for the in-depth discussions you're longing to have about the perineum and Pitocin, so it's best not to go back to that well too frequently or you'll burn him out before birthing class even gets started. Let a sister be your guide.

RULE #10:
Don't take in stuff that scares you.

When I was first pregnant, I made the brain-dead mistake of watching the movie *The Fly*. In case you've never enjoyed this riveting remake of the Vincent Price cult classic, it's the story of a woman whose mad-scientist boyfriend attempts to transport himself through space, but accidentally gets trapped in the time machine with a fly. (I hate when that happens.) Before she realizes the inevitable outcome of this mishap, the boyfriend impregnates her, suffers through a gruesome descent into flyhood, and dies. Of course, nine months later she gives birth to . . . well, you know where this is going.

wendy's wisdom from across the waters

In England, we don't have this American obsession about total absti-nence. Nor do we take on the quest for perfection in our children. I think the end result is that we're more relaxed about our pregnan-cies—having a bit of wine with dinner if we feel like it—and more realistic about the fact that things sometimes can and do go tragically wrong. And that occurrence is not divine retribution being exacted on the mum for naughty behavior during pregnancy, when she was a teenager, or whatever. I think Americans are very hard-core about this and it's not a particularly healthy or attractive quality.

That movie freaked me out for about three months, point-lessly and needlessly, since Mr. Wrong was clearly a dog, not a fly. Anyhow, my rule of thumb about this is pretty simple. If what you're reading or watching (*60 Minutes,*

a few words on weed, whites, and wine

Speaking of pot . . . don't. This is obviously a no-brainer and I shouldn't have to reiterate it, but I will, because it's so critically important. I can tell you of three or four women I know who thought it might be a good idea to keep up their party profile during pregnancy (drinking, smoking pot, snorting cocaine, or all of the above), and those kids are a mess. ADD. ADHD. BAD. It's no joke. And it's certainly not worth it. So if you think being good to yourself includes imbibing, forget it. For the nine months it takes to build a beautiful, healthy baby, you can stay stone-cold sober. Besides, ramping down your party appetite now is going to stand you in good stead for the complete lack of a life you'll have when the Precious Bundle appears and opens its precious rosebud mouth.

that new serial killer mystery, or your husband's cooking) makes you clutch your little tummy and start breathing with harsh panicky gasps, get away from it. Pregnancy is scary enough without adding anything else to the pot.

Move into positive, as Bob Marley would say. And stay there.

RULE #11:
Be the life of the party!
Suddenly, you are on everybody's A list. No party is complete unless you're there. Bachelorette celebration? Yours is the first

invitation in the mail. Yes, there's nothing like a reliable, can't-squirm-out-of-it, won't-decide-a-few-cosmos-don't count, die-hard designated driver to make any fete more fun. To be more specific, because you're now relentlessly sober, you're the life of everybody *else*'s party. Don't let this hurt your feelings. Just make yourself useful and go with the flow. It may not be the raucous, wild-and-crazy old you out there dancing on top of the bar, but it might prove surprising to discover how much fun you can have without the help of anything but your hormones. And oh, the secrets you'll learn when the *vino* brings out the *veritas*. Be discreet, even if it kills you. (Remember: Revealed Secrets + Desire to Keep You Quiet = Major Baby Gift.)

RULE #12:
Wake up and smell the . . . oh, never mind.
For most women, the first trimester of pregnancy is spent in a woozy, snoozy fog. Personally, I was on mega-high alert for signs of miscarriage, so sleep was a dim luxury that loomed somewhere just out of my grasp. But my hope is that your life is far less harrowing. And thanks to the hormones flooding your system, you'll probably feel the need for a few extra hours of sleep every couple of minutes. Which is *fine*. Your body will tell you what it needs. In fact, the one thing that becomes crystal clear in pregnancy is You Are Not In Control. So give in to those heavy eyelids, grab a pillow, and hit the hay. Consciousness is totally overrated.

RULE #13:
Repeat after me.
Whenever you're feeling a little blue (thanks to the onslaught of hormones), place your hand on your belly and whisper these two little words:

My baby. (repeat)
My baby. (repeat)
My baby.

It's a mantra for pregnancy peace and happiness.

Bonus Pointer for High-Achieving Moms:
There was only one Einstein.
I know this is heresy (and $165 million in annual sales might prove me wrong), but I don't really believe that playing a bunch of musical tapes for your baby in utero or in the nursery is going to make a significant difference in the child's intelligence. When Lulu was two, a brilliant and witty friend of mine was expecting his first child and became convinced that if he played classical music to his wife's womb every day, the child would be able to speak in full sentences before reaching the age of one. As any mother of a two-year-old can tell you, the magic of speech loses a bit of its luster once the child has achieved formidable mastery of the words *No! Will not!* and *You're not the boss of me!* Naturally, you begin to wonder what you were in such a hurry to foster.

Nevertheless, my friend kept up the symphonic tutorials throughout his wife's pregnancy (although I felt that all that attention to his baby's intelligence might have been focused more productively on his choice of the other provider of genetic material, as the mother was—how can I put this delicately?—a complete moron). My friend's child is now eight and adorable but not, thank God, a genius. Nor was he a prodigy of early speech.

I can totally understand the urge to get the jump on early childhood development, but all these new baby intelligence products make me wonder if there isn't something slightly egotistical and perhaps a tad unhealthy about trying to impact our kids' SAT scores before they even get their APGARs. At the risk of sounding completely old school, it seems to me that while we're working so diligently to make certain our children are advanced, we should take equal care to be sure we're not fast-forwarding through their one and only childhood. Of course, this kind of equanimity is almost impossible to maintain once you begin to hear parents around you rumbling with sophisticated, savvy plans for ratcheting up their infant's brainpower while your Precious Bundle appears to have hit a plateau at learning to swallow his fist. Take a deep, cleansing breath and keep in mind that child prodigies are born, not created. And P.S.: Genius doesn't come with a soundtrack.

CHAPTER TWO

Pregnancy Rules: 3 to 6 Months— Middle Earth

i feel pretty, oh so pretty . . .

Generally speaking, this is the good stage of pregnancy. You've stopped throwing up, you actually look pregnant and not like the new Plus Size prototype, and you haven't yet swelled up to the size of a zeppelin. Enjoy it while it lasts, babe. Seriously, while you still have your energy, your emotional equilibrium, and the ability to see your toes, get busy.

Perhaps by this, you think I mean it's time to get your layette together. (What *is* a layette, anyhow? And why do they make those dumb layette lists, as if everybody should have all the same stuff? I could never understand why I needed ten little baby washcloths when you couldn't possibly use more than two in the first place. And what's up with those sleepers with the drawstring bottom? It's like your kid is a head of lettuce.) Nope, I'm not talking about putting together the layette here. Save all that nesting stuff for your last trimester, when you're going to develop an insane urge to paint, reupholster, and move large pieces of furniture around. Now is the time to strut around looking fecund and fertile, flaunting your pregnancy for all the world to see. In short, now's the time to have some F-U-N.

Herewith, Twelve Fat-Free Tips for a First-Rate Second Trimester.

RULE #14:
Get outta here. (Part I)

Take a road trip someplace dumb, like Wyoming. Stay in a cheap motel and watch movies until really late, sleep in, then go out for a huge stack of pancakes and bacon at a local diner. Go back to the motel and take a ridiculously long bath, using up every towel in the room. Don't make the bed or even attempt to tidy up. Get back on the road and repeat until satisfied.

The idea here is to violate every domestic routine you can, without having to clean up after yourself—and catch a big old tantalizing breath of freedom while you're at it. If you've got the wherewithal, you can always grab a flight to someplace exotic while they'll still let you on the plane, but I prefer road trips for the sheer James Dean/*Thelma & Louise* romance of it all. Road trips, by definition, make you feel bohemian, untethered, and full of infinite possibility—all sentiments, I can assure you, that will become as foreign as Swahili in another three months.

RULE #15:
Enjoy your breasts.

Okay, this may only apply to women like me who never got anything but As (and I'm not talking about high-school chemistry here). But the chance to have big, firm, bouncing, glorious, voluptuous breasts, not to mention cleavage!—well, that deserves some kind of jubilee.

I suggest a full swoon of shopping in the intimate apparel department. Even if you're heading straight back to an A-cup the nanosecond your breastfeeding days are over, you might as well enjoy this brief foray into busty-ness and outfit yourself accordingly. Lace is good. Sheer lace is great. Strapless is excellent, as long as your cup is not runneth-ing too far over. And should you wander over into the Reckless Decolletage/Maternity Slut section of the dress department (if only!), don't let us stop you.

Of course, if you already started out well-endowed (bitch) and have now moved into the southern regions of the alphabet—like my friend Clarice, who had to send away to Frederick's of Hollywood for her Gs (at first I thought she meant "strings," and couldn't believe she was still feeling so frisky)—well, it's still important that your abundant breasts be well supported and gorgeously clad during your pregnancy. And the sooner, the better. Your boobs are going to be completely upstaged by your belly in a matter of weeks, so give them their day in the sun.

Although if you're going to take that literally, don't forget to break out the sunblock.

RULE #16:
Buy new sheets.

Pretty soon now, you're going to develop some real problems getting the full dose of slumber you need. Unless you've developed an aptitude for sleeping on a basketball, you're going to have to sleep on your side while someone kicks you all night. This stage will be accompanied by the stress of trying to sleep while someone constantly awakens you for feeding, comforting, and reassurance. (That's just your partner's way of getting attention before the baby comes—at which point, the real night games of feeding, comforting, and nurturing will begin.) This Insomnizoic Era will last for approximately the next twelve years. Clearly, you're going to need all the help you can get in achieving anything close to eight hours of blessed, restorative sleep per night.

A lovely bed can help. In fact, I honestly and earnestly believe that nice sheets can change your life (but then, I did spend a good part of my life in advertising). In fact, it was an ad of a beautifully rumpled bed and a headline that queried, "It's one-third of your life. Why not spend it in Wamsutta luxury?" that utterly brainwashed me and led me down this path to the boudoir. Now whenever I'm truly depressed or blue, I buy new sheets. But it's a mild addiction. Making a beautiful bed is a gift to yourself, and I urge every woman to try it. If you look for sales, this doesn't even have to be a budget whacker. And it is *one-third of your life* that you actually have a chance of improving through shopping. What a concept!

RULE #17:

Get a move on.

Sometime during the fourth month, you are going to feel your baby move for the very first time. This is a heart-stopping moment (well, not literally). The instant you first feel your baby move, it means that all the ultrasounds and doctors' appointments and weight gain and morning sickness weren't just a cruel hoax to make you believe you're pregnant. It's cold, beautiful proof that you *are* pregnant. There is something in there, by God! And it's moving, it's doing backflips, it's fine and dandy. This is *major.*

I was so eager to get this telegram from my tummy, I would lie on my back for hours, hoping to bring it on. But what would it feel like? What if my baby was in there, tumbling around like a trapeze artist, and I was just too unenlightened and insensitive to know? What if it was lying around in my uterus like some tiny baby slacker, purposely withholding all movement just to drive me nuts?

My friend Mimi told me, "Honestly, Betty, you'll know it the minute you feel it. It's an unmistakable sensation, like someone lightly running a fingernail down the inside of your stomach." That was a little esoteric for me, but then, I have left no nail unbitten, so it's fair to say I have no idea how one might feel.

Finally, one morning, just as I was waking up, on vacation in a quiet house in Sanibel, Florida, I felt it! But it didn't feel like a fingernail at all. It felt like a fish flipping over in the water. An undulating sort of motion, like when you drive over a bump too fast and for a few seconds your tires leave the road and you're suspended in air. That was Lulu's first message to me. I'm heeeerrrrrrrreeeeeeeee. Pure bliss. (Of course, in four months when your baby starts doing The Wave inside your womb and your stomach begins to resemble Sigourney Weaver's in *Alien*, you probably won't appreciate the baby's movement quite so much, but that's way down the road.)

RULE #18:
Unplug the name drain.

Have you picked a name yet?
Have you picked a name yet?
Have you picked a name yet?

Perhaps in an attempt to stave off any physical pregnancy information you might be inclined to share (like your fear of an episiotomy or your propensity to develop painful hemorrhoids), people may try to engage you in a conversation about names before you've even come to terms with the idea that there's really a kid in there. Don't get sucked in by this gambit.

Even if you are one of those annoying overachievers who have actually settled on a name for your child before normal people like me even put it on the "To Do" list, it makes no sense whatsoever to share it with others. (This goes triple for any immediate family members who are already likely to feel overinvested in the process. Unless you really are going to include them in the decision—check your spine first—it's cruel to give them the illusion that they will be fully enfranchised voters in this election.) For starters, if people like the name you've chosen, you'll immediately have to decide if you trust their taste. What does the inside of their house look like? Are they tchotchke people? Cheerful hangers of holiday flags? What if they clearly possess utterly pedestrian taste *and* like the name you've chosen? Should you abandon that name and start all over? (*Answer*: Of course.)

On the other hand, some people seem to have a genuine yet mystifying need to give you their honest appraisal of the name *you've* chosen for *your* child (note pronouns). "Gosh, I don't remember asking for your opinion," would be an appropriate, if churlish, response when someone trash-talks your chosen name, but believe me, you'll be stewing over every word of criticism in your mind at 3 A.M. Even the most die-hard free-thinker may feel cowed by the responsibility of giving a child a name that may bring on years of playground abuse, middle school snickers, and canceled high school prom dates, not to mention rendering the aforementioned child permanently unemployable.

Of course, waiting until the last minute to choose a name does have its downside. Lulu wasn't named until eighteen excruciating days after her birth, while I tried out one name after another, attempting to find one that fit. She was Charlotte for a couple of days (too formal), Madeline for a couple of days (too whimsical), Chloe for a half hour (too precious), then in rapid succession, Daisy, Lily, and Caroline. Friends who called became a bit testy when they'd jovially open with,

"So how's little Chloe?" and I'd reply in a postpartum fog of forgetfulness, "Sorry, wrong room," and hang up on them.

If you'd like to avoid these shenanigans and browse ahead, you can always check out last year's most popular names for boys and girls on the Social Security Administration's Web site. However, if you remember the dreaded Jennifer phenomenon that washed over the 1980s like a plague of locusts, I would personally avoid these. Then again, I named my kid Lulu. 'Nuff said.

celebrity baby names available for copying

Amandine
John Malkovich

Assisi
Jade Jagger

Apple
Gwyneth Paltrow

Blue Angel
Dave Evans (AKA The Edge, from U2)

Brooklyn, Romeo, and Cruz
David Beckham

Chester and Truman
Tom Hanks and Rita Wilson

Cosima
Nigella Lawson

Milo
Ricky Lake

Racer, Rebel, and Rocket
Robert Rodriguez

Seven
Erykah Badu

Taj
Steven Tyler

emma (better known as chopsy) makes the call

When Betty was trying to decide on a name a week or so after Lulu's birth, she called me (in England), sobbing. She really wanted to name her daughter Lulu, but everybody was giving her a hard time about it. "My ex thinks it sounds like a Vegas stripper," she hiccupped, "the Texas grandparents think it means 'mistake,' and my friend Bevan says that a name gives a critical first impression of a person and if I name my daughter Lulu, everybody will think she is frivolous." "Well for godsakes, I *hope* she's frivolous!" I hollered over the transatlantic cable. "Being frivolous means being joyful, irrepressible and full of fun. It's a fabulous name!" And that was how Lulu became Lulu.

RULE #19:
Keep it clean.

Normally, I don't give advice on housekeeping. My theory is that you're either a slob or a neatnik and nothing is going to change that. (And slobs only marry neatniks and vice versa, just to ensure the lifelong torture of one's mate.) However, if you can establish the habits of keeping a neat house now, it's going to serve you well in the coming years of purgatory also known as parenthood. In fact, you've got nine months to shape up, sister, or you will never, ever see the bottom of your closet again. Am I making myself clear?

A clean house is a sign of self-respect, and it's something you can give yourself every day of your life if you so choose. So choose. If you're one of the truly troubled, go to the *www.flylady.com*

Web site, which is sort of an AA for slobs. I understand that it's a really good how-to site (and now a book called *Sink Reflections*) to help you wrestle your house back into a semblance of order. Check it out. Snap on those rubber gloves. And get going.

sarah's slobbing-out rule

Betty is an insanely obsessive housekeeper. Pay no attention at all to what she says. This is actually the perfect time to start training yourself to become oblivious to the chaos into which your house will descend once the little darling appears. Trying to keep it spotless will only drive you crazy (like Betty), so get in training now. Practice denial. Throw towels on the floor and purposely ignore them. Get out a stopwatch or calendar and see how long you can walk over objects without actually picking them up. Squint and see how pretty everything suddenly appears. Go blind to dust. In fact, contemplate what Quentin Crisp advised: If you let the dust collect for five years, it will never get any deeper than that. Imagine your floors wall-to-wall and knee-deep in My Little Ponys and Polly Pockets; then look at what you're currently dealing with and be grateful. Why, your house is practically immaculate!

RULE #20:
Don't let them tell you how much you weigh.

If you're anything like I am—shallow, vain, and insecure (or simply American and female)—you probably have an issue with your weight. Pregnancy does not offer a respite from this burden. Instead, as you're packing on the pounds, you're also going to be forced to go in and get weighed every couple of weeks.

As a general rule, I never let myself get weighed. My very admirably assertive friend Mimi was the first one to enlighten me that they can't actually make you step on the scales in a general checkup, and I've never looked back. At the doctor's office, my chart has a cranky "Refuses to be Weighed" complaint emblazoned right on the cover.

But your OB isn't going to let you get away with that crap. You're going to get weighed every visit, like it or not. However, they don't have to share that information with you. You can close your eyes as Nurse Ratchet taps that little weight further and further to the right, past 140, 145, 150—and make her promise not to tell you. Now naturally, the doctor is going to ride your ever-widening butt if you've gone completely over the recommended weight gain, but you might be able to strike a deal that unless it's a problem, they won't tell you. The nurses may not be sympathetic participants in this scheme, but I've found they can generally recognize a volatile lunatic when they see one.

So just ask. Ignorance is bliss. Take back the power!

RULE #21:
Break out the cute stuff.
I hate to be the bearer of heavy tidings, but right now, you're hitting the peak of your pregnancy appeal. And it's a godawful luge ride downhill from here. So don't wait a second longer

to wear all the flirty, fun, and sassy clothes you can still cram yourself into. If you've got great legs, by all means, break out the thigh-high boots and pregnancy suede mini. If you've got that Kate Hudson thing going, slip right into that cropped-top-and-bare-tummy look. You can work it, you can shake it like a Polaroid picture, and everybody will still think you're all that, Miss Thing. But in a few weeks, the gig will be up. Big, serious pregnancy is moving in like an Arctic cold front, and at that point, it's going to be all about coverage. Sure, you can take a page from Catherine Zeta-Jones's book and still choose to flaunt your spectacular cleavage, but the rest of you is best treated as a Christo project and artfully wrapped in fabric. Miles and miles of it. (Belly Basics, the fashionistas of chic pregnancy clothes, swear that even women with not-so-great legs will find their gams look spectacularly slim and shapely throughout pregnancy, due to the counterbalance of the unwieldy lump hovering above. I say, dream on.)

RULE #22:
Consider not knowing.
Right about now, you can find out the sex of your baby. Some people can't stand the suspense. Personally, since I felt destined to be an overinvolved mother for the rest of my kid's life, I figured my baby deserved the privacy of those nine months in the womb, during which time I would be relatively unable to form any preconceived notions about who he/she was, and what the hell he/she was doing in there. That seemed fair. Mr. Wrong

also had a surprisingly lucid point of view on this. He was adamant about not knowing, claiming that it was one of life's truly great surprises and would be something to look forward to during the long hours of labor. And that was true. But you're going to have to be steadfastly *committed* to not knowing because the nurses (bless their hearts) really, really want to tell you.

I was getting an ultrasound in about my sixth month, and the nurse asked me—for the fifth time—if I wanted to know what it was. ("Just not a puppy," I prayed, still haunted by my cinematic encounter with *The Fly*.) Wavering with curiosity, I said, "I don't think I want to know." Quick as can be, she swung the screen around to face me, announcing gleefully, "I'm looking right at it!" Luckily, the picture on the ultrasound resembled an Etch A Sketch gone terribly wrong, and I couldn't pick out anything that looked remotely human, much less definitively male or female. The secret was safe. In my mind, Lulu remained a cute, chubby little boy named Augustus Homer for the entire nine months. (Lulu loves this story—especially the part where she doesn't get saddled with a totally lame name.)

Do whatever feels right, but don't choose to find out just because you can. Give it some thought.

cecily's knowing discourse

The above advice is coming to you from the Queen of Delayed Gratification—a woman who's never *once* opened a birthday card or a Christmas present before the actual holiday. However, I am a normal impatient person, and think it makes perfect sense to find out the sex of your baby as soon as you possibly can—if only to avoid *my* gender-bender experience. I was a young mom, and didn't have an amniocentesis, but early on, the nurse told me from the ultrasound she was sure I was having a girl. So I went out and bought all pink clothes, painted the nursery a girly color, and got all frothy, feminine bedding. When Harry—not Harriet—was born, it was quite a surprise. Of course, my husband was convinced that his little son was going to grow up to star in *La Cage aux Folles* if he didn't rush right out and get him appropriately masculine little sports jerseys and rough-and-tumble cowboy curtains. We had a boatload of redecorating and shopping to do on the fly.

Today, ultrasound technology is far more accurate and it's easy to find out for sure, so why wait? Then you can use those six months to choose a name, decorate the nursery, buy baby clothes that aren't gender-neutral yellow, and start developing a gender-appropriate relationship with the little critter.

RULE #23:
Beware the nutrition nazis.

My favorite book when I was pregnant was *What to Expect When You're Expecting*. Since I never expected to be among the ranks of the expecting, I was delighted beyond description to be able to legitimately buy the book. I loved every chapter and tried to religiously follow each word of advice. I even rushed out to the local bookstore and bought a copy of the companion tome, *What to Eat When You're Expecting*. Big mistake. For starters, the cover alone is terrifying: A grown-up Heidi, tucked into a dirndl skirt,

CHEC This Out

I am not an alarmist and God knows, nobody has ever accused me of clean living, but right now, you need to be sure that your house and environment are as toxin-free as possible. The Children's Health Environmental Coalition (CHEC) is an organization that was started by an amazing woman who lost a child to cancer, and is dedicated to educating parents about everyday chemicals and substances that pose a substantial risk to children, before and after birth. CHEC has a rocking Web site crammed with stuff you really need to know. Bleach, carpet cleaners, air fresheners, and common cleaners have all been implicated in childhood cancers, asthma, and serious health issues that also pose grave developmental danger to expecting mothers. Even if we adults can cope with all the chemicals, pesticides, and toxins that surround us (which is questionable), newborn babies are infinitely more susceptible to the onslaught. If you visit the Web site, CHEC will even send you a free e-mail newsletter with age-appropriate tips. It's a simple, essential homework assignment for expecting moms. Go to *www.checnet.org* and get smart.

holds a huge mixing bowl, looking beatific and 100 percent natural. There I was, sitting in the food court, reading the first chapter, about the dangers of sugar. Any sugar. All sugar. Sugar was bad.

The Cinnabon clutched in my fist took on gargantuan, ghastly proportions. What had I eaten for breakfast? Oh yeah, French toast. Great. My baby's brain was probably awash in deadly sucrose right at that very moment. Gestational diabetes was no doubt a single mouthful away! Just then I think my mother's spirit must have entered me, and I thought, "Hold your horses there, missy. Pregnant women have been eating sugar for centuries. And I'm supposed to be putting apricot purée on wholewheat pancakes? I don't think so." I walked right back into the store, got a big old refund, and got on with my sweet pregnancy.

You don't have to get crazy and totalitarian about your diet just because you're trying to do the right thing. Pregnancy is a lot about losing control over your body, and giving in to that change, which is great. But you don't have to give up *everything*. Just be smart, be moderate, and be good to yourself. My favorite treat when I was pregnant (vegetarians, please skip immediately to the next Rule) was a Big Bite hot dog from 7-11, slathered in chili, cheese, onions, relish, ketchup, mustard, and peppers. When I got finished at the complimentary condiment bar, I could hardly lift the thing. It never failed to cheer me up on those rare occasions when I could summon the courage to sidle in and carry out something destined to make me even larger. Oh well. Sometimes a little of the wrong stuff is exactly what you need. (But please reread "A Few Words on Weed, Whites, and Wine" in Chapter 1 first.)

shani's vegan variation on the theme

I've been really careful about what I eat for years, and the fact that I'm pregnant—and totally psyched about it—only makes me want to be more conscious that I'm eating right. (Betty wanted me to tell you that I'm also a skydiver and base jumper so you won't think this advice is coming from some hypercautious, risk-averse chick. My fear is of *frying*, not flying.) Since I'm a vegan, I have to be really conscious that I'm getting enough protein, calcium, and folic acid, but it's really not that difficult to eat healthily. A vegan friend who just had a baby brought over a huge bottle of unsulfored molasses, which has gobs of good stuff in it. I'm eating tofu, protein shakes, rice, beans, nuts, drinking lots of pregnancy teas and juices, and taking all the pregnancy vitamins like B12, folic acid, and calcium. Personally, I feel so much better when I eat good food, I don't know why anybody would choose to eat junk. No offense, but Betty is totally out to lunch on this one. So to speak.

(Betty's rebuttal: *Sorry, still doesn't touch a Cinnabon.*)

RULE #24:
Stretched thin?

Well actually, you're stretched and you're getting fatter by the minute. The question here is: What can one do to avoid stretch marks? All the books say that you're either genetically predisposed or you're not—so lotions, potions, and prayers aren't going to make a shred of difference in whether you end up with those silvery reminders of the astonishing lengths (and widths) to which you went for your Precious Bundle. But I'm not buying it. I'm a big believer in cocoa butter, probably because it was my mother's favorite, and she made it through eight pregnancies without a mark. (Wrinkly stomach skin is another story but hey, something had to give.) I also believe in liberal amounts of Vitamin E and orange essential oil, sprinkled in your bath water with some calming lavender, because it's supposed to have skin-healing properties. The goal is to keep your skin full of moisture and try not to gain too much weight. In other words, don't turn the basketball you're carrying into a watermelon. *Capisce?*

RULE #25:
Find your "floor."
The first time I heard about my pelvic floor muscles, I was pretty sure that I had good ones. That confidence turned out to be sadly misplaced. To be honest (and I hope I won't offend anyone here), I've never been exactly clear just where my pelvic floor is, although I'm sure it's down there somewhere. As for recent books that suggest "working the deep transversus abdominis to prevent diastasis" (sounds like Greek to me, too), I suspect I would need OnStar tracking capabilities to find that abdominal muscle, much less work it out. And the kegel exercises they sternly admonish you to practice? Forget about it. Oh yeah, I can squeeze the muscles around the vagina and stop the flow of urine, but I know I'm not doing a real kegel because your butt muscles aren't supposed to be involved at

all, and mine are clenched tighter than a vise grip. When I sheepishly admitted this to my OB, he suggested I go in for biofeedback sessions three times a week to practice, but there's a limit to the amount of time I'm willing to devote to my kegels (as opposed to the almost unlimited time I'm eager to devote to bagels). Basically, I hit the floor. But I'm sure you're a much better mother than I, and will quickly learn how to draw in the transverse to compress the abdominal cavity during labor contractions and relax the pelvic floor to slide the baby out. (And yes, it's just that simple!)

Bonus Pointer for Sole Proprietors:
Make some gay friends.

If you're a single mother, having some male gay friends is probably going to save your life. First of all, they're funny. I don't think I have a single gay friend who doesn't have a superb sense of humor and somehow manages to grasp the ridiculous and hilarious paradox of everyday life. And let's face it: It's a lot healthier to be able to laugh at cruel twists of fate, like the simultaneous onset of acne and wrinkles, than it is to sob endlessly about it.

Second, gay guys are still *guys,* so they can help you understand the pathological psychology of their kind. For example, they can translate the mysterious language of men and explain that when a guy says, "I love you but I'm just not ready to commit," he really means, "I'm not in love with you at all, but I still want to sleep with you because you'll let me." Helpful things like that, to keep you and the Precious Bundle from falling into the clutches of yet another Mr. Not-Quite-Right.

Your gay friends will also help you stay on top of your fashion game—telling you with blinding clarity just how terrible that leopard-skin coat with the huge shoulder pads makes you look. But they'll do it in a *kind* way, unlike many of your girlfriends, who secretly revel in your serial fashion faux pas.

Finally, *my* male gay friends (I don't want to make generalizations here—whoops, a little late for that) are incredibly tender-hearted, sweet, and loyal guys who will stand by you in your hour(s) of need, celebrate the incredible journey of pregnancy with you, and delight with joy in your fabulous offspring. In short, they're everything a man should be.

CHAPTER THREE

Pregnancy Rules: 7 to 9 Months— The Final Stretch

just shoot me

Wᵉ're not going to sugarcoat it. This is the pathetic part of pregnancy. You're huge. You waddle. Your emotions are tsunamic. And you're a tremulous, heaving bundle of neediness. It's okay; it's supposed to be like this! That way, when you actually give birth, you don't mind going through the indescribable agonies of labor, staying up with a sleepless baby for forty-eight consecutive hours, or having milk shoot out of your breasts all over your nice silk shirt. It's a relief! At least you're not pregnant anymore.

My due date was Mother's Day. I spent the day taking care of Mr. Wrong's bored-to-death five-year-old daughter and doing a bit of grocery shopping. While I was carrying the bags into the house, one dropped, and a bottle of Claussen Dill Pickles (I am not making this up) shattered on the tiles, slicing my little toe almost in two. I'd never seen blood shoot out of an artery or vein before and I was astonished to see what a vigorous, arching spray resulted. Attempting to stanch the flow of blood before it could further gross out Mr. Wrong's daughter, who was now screaming at the top of her lungs, I waddled rapidly into the bathroom and sat in the tub. Unfortunately, since I was two or three times my normal width, I got stuck in the tub and had to ask her to stop yelping and help pry me out. We drove to the hospital and I got fifteen stitches in my toe. Then I couldn't wear shoes. Ergo, I was barefoot, pregnant, and overdue.

The next week, eight days overdue, I decided to take a brisk walk in an attempt to induce labor. I tripped on my flip-flops, right over a curb I couldn't see (because my stomach was in the way), and fell into the street, where I could barely get up (because my stomach was in the way). As I limped home, sobbing wildly, with bloody knees, torn pants, and ripped flip-flops, I realized I was never, ever going to have this baby. I was going to be this hideously pregnant forever.

I tell this story not just for your amusement or to make you feel smugly superior (as in, "Wow, what a totally pathetic cow. At least I'll never let myself sink that low!"), but to prove how truly challenging the last wheezing gasps of pregnancy can be. It is therefore imperative that you do your level best to find some way—any way—to hold on to your relentlessly deteriorating self-image and keep the faith that there is Life After Baby.

Here are Twelve Ports in the Storm.

RULE #26:
Wear anything that fits.

When I was five months pregnant and still full of jaunty confidence that I was going to be adorable for the entire nine months, my friend Mimi offered to lend me the maternity dress she affectionately referred to as "Big Red." It was big. And it was red. Red-and-white striped, in fact. It looked like an awning. There was no way I was ever going to be that big. In fact, I felt a little sorry for Mimi that she'd ever let herself go like that.

Fast-forward three months. My brother was getting married. I had nothing that fit. I swallowed my pride (along with a couple of Donut Gems), called Mimi, and asked for Big Red. And now there's a family wedding album in which I closely resemble a festive circus tent. Oh well. Just roll with it. By month eight, no matter which way you turn or what you put on, you're going to look like a beached whale. So relinquish the struggle and let yourself go.

You don't really have a choice anyhow. Ever seen pictures of Gwyneth, Kate, Madonna, and Elizabeth Hurley when they were in their final days of pregnancy? They had thunder thighs. Their faces were swollen balloons. They looked . . . pregnant! Now if the best bodies in the world can't fight it, who are you? Give into hugeness. Buy the flowered muumuu. Break out the paisley tent dress from high school. Wear your husband's pants—you'll feel almost svelte, and as an added bonus, he'll probably be highly irritated by it. Whatever gets you through the next couple of weeks (they will surely feel like years) . . . put it on.

RULE #27:
Nest away.

There comes a time in every woman's pregnancy when she will feel a pressing need to prepare her home for the baby. That time is NOW! RIGHT NOW! I MEAN, RIGHT THIS FREAKING MINUTE!!! Yes, in this last trimester of pregnancy, the urge to "nest" can hardly be overstated.

A quiet and mild-mannered friend of mine, who weighs about 95 pounds on a bloated water-weight day, single-handedly wrestled a 150-pound solid walnut rocking chair out of the back of her Subaru after a marathon shopping-for-baby trip. While performing this feat, Kristi (who attends church more regularly than Jerry Falwell) was swearing up such a storm, the young children next door were immediately herded indoors. The real culprit? Her 200-pound gym teacher husband who had decided, unwisely, to take a breather and watch a bit of the Broncos game before unloading the car. Kristi was about sixty-five weeks pregnant at the time. She delivered the next day.

My own sweet sister Bonnie, equally piqued by her man's disinterest in furniture rearrangement, decided to take things into her own hands. One Sunday afternoon while she was prowling around the living room looking for things to improve, she realized that her perfectly nice sofa was completely unacceptable in the home where her darling baby would soon reside. A woman of action, Bonnie picked up that full-length sofa and, when she couldn't shove it out the door, lifted it up and shoved it out the living room window. Needless to say, about halfway through, the sofa got stuck, and despite several people's subsequent efforts to remove it, there it remained hanging forlornly for more than two weeks. In January. In Colorado. A couple of days later, Bonnie gave birth to a beautiful baby girl who is still a sweet and adorable child, so all I can say is that clearly she got rid of that sofa just in time.

My point here is this: There's no fighting the gravitational pull of nature to nest, so it's best to just give in. This advice goes double or triple for the five men reading this. Get out your tool belt, your checkbook, and your jumping shoes, and then practice saying, "How high, honey?" until you sound at least a tiny bit sincere. Very good. You may live to see the birth yet.

RULE #28:
Watch the cesarean section movie—just in case.
I went to Lamaze training with my hilarious British friend, Bevan. I had really wanted Mr. Wrong to go with me, and we actually made it through one whole class, which I spent massaging his back. But when he informed me that he might not be able to make it to the actual birth, I figured I'd better develop a backup plan. Bevan stepped right up and proved to be a very entertaining labor coach during our practice sessions together. On the night they showed the movie explaining when and how a cesarean section might be done, Bevan and I were cracking jokes together in the back of the class, sharing creative ways to cut people open and other immature repartee. It never occurred to me that I would have a c-section, as I come from a family of women who pop out babies like

human Pez dispensers. My mom had eight children, with no anesthesia. My four sisters never even opted for the epidural. Even my sisters-in-law were paragons of natural childbirth. Of course, I didn't share any of their disdain for pain relief, but no way was I going to get cut open. Well, pride goeth before a fall, as they say. And I fell into that growing group of women who made the cut. Watch the movie. You never know.

mimi's fat-free rule

When my doctor told me I was going to have a c-section, I could only think of one thing. My second-best shallow friend, when she had her c-section, had her doctor scrape about five pounds of fat from her tummy while he was in there. Bonus! A side of liposuction with your c-section! Of course, my doctor was a big killjoy and looked at me like I was overdosing on Häagen-Dazs when I suggested it, but I thought it was a *great* idea. Anyhow, a few words about c-sections and mother/baby bonding. You're going to have hundreds of thousands of hours to bond with the Precious Bundle, and the first twenty minutes of life are not going to make or break your relationship. Trust me. It'll take adolescence to accomplish that. If you get the c-section, you'll be able to lie around, watch TV, and order the nurses around for five extra days. I highly recommend that.

RULE #29:
Head for the shower.

Let's be honest here. Baby showers, unless there's a lot of alcohol involved, are really only fun for the mother-to-be. But having suffered through dozens of bridal and baby showers through the years, you've more than earned the right to lord over the festivities on the day when you get to star in your very own. Don't be bashful about asking for what you really want. Women who are not actively knocked up do not want to go in a baby store and browse—give them a task, let them complete it and move straight on to Neiman Marcus, where they can look at Bobbi Brown's new eye shadows and forget you exist.

Of course, the $6 billion American baby products industry has made it a point to promote baby registries so you can choose exactly what you want (and three times more than you could possibly use), but I'm not quite certain I'm up for that level of specificity. Call me old-fashioned, but I think baby registries are a tiny bit *rude,* since you will, de facto, know precisely what every person spent on you and that is just not good manners, as my dear mother would say. However, it's up to you. I just would try to reign in your enthusiasm for some of the more gadgety baby products out there, because when the Precious Bundle arrives you'll quickly discover that a) you don't have time to promote the dazzling array of new products to him/her, you just need something that works; quick! and b) the more stuff you have, the more you'll have to lug around, put away, and generally manage—and time management is something that evaporates within the first few hours of motherhood.

Technically, I didn't actually require a baby shower. My fabulous friend Michelle had already given me almost every baby accoutrement known to woman. (She is also one of the original Shallow Moms whom I adore, since she is not only a great mother but an unerringly truthful one. The first time I saw her nursing, she lay back on her sofa with an exasperated sigh, shifted baby Bryan from one breast to another and, looking up at me from under a gorgeous tangle of blonde curls said conspiratorially, "Motherhood sucks, Betty. Literally. They're just here to suck the life out of you." Then she laughed and went back to cuddling her son.)

My equally fabulous friend Clarice threw my baby shower, which right away assured record attendance. Clarice's house was amazing; her outfit—as always—featured a breathtaking abundance of cleavage; her alcohol selection was huge; and the food surprisingly delicious. Clarice looks like a Victoria's Secret model, has the flamboyant style of Frida Kahlo, the kick-ass energy of Uma Thurman, the mouth of Joan Rivers, and is one of those intimidating Sewing Women who can whip up a roomful of floor-to-ceiling curtains in an afternoon. But in all my years of knowing her, I've only seen Clarice cook one dish. Chicken Chili. Her Chicken Chili is incredible, unless she happens to drink too much vodka while cooking, in which case it is completely inedible. This was one of her sober cooking days and the chili rocked, although I confined myself to a spoonful to avoid the dreaded heartburn conflagration. About fifty women showed up. The party went on for hours. I got everything. People were incredibly generous.

See pages 48–49 for Clarice's secret recipe.

kyoko's right of excess

My husband and I tried for years to get pregnant. I used to walk by the baby stores and think: I am never, ever going to get to go in there and buy all that adorable stuff. So when it finally happened, and I now have a great big pregnant belly that gives me the right of entry, I'm not about to deny myself anything! I love all the gadgets, the clothes, the furniture, the necessities, and the ridiculous excess. Honestly? I've never had more fun spending money, and I couldn't care less if it's extravagant. The $200 video nursery monitor—check! The ultimate $799 stroller—a must! A Prada diaper bag—naturally! I'm having more fun shopping for all this baby stuff than I ever had shopping for myself, and you know what? I earned it! We went through hell and heartbreak getting to this point, and now all I have to say is, "See you at the register!"

RULE #30:
See the pillow. Be the pillow.

No matter how much you work out, pregnancy is nature's way of turning the hardest hard body into a pillow. (Okay, I don't know this to be true in *every* case, since my exercise schedule was a tiny bit sketchy during pregnancy.) But it makes a lot of sense. A baby doesn't want to curl up under six-pack abs, or have to lay its little head on a bony hip. A baby wants a fluffy, puffy pillow and what baby wants, baby gets. (Did you know that if you don't get enough calcium when you're pregnant, the baby will leech it right out of your gums and teeth? It's true—they're little vampires!)

Clarice's **Intoxicating Chicken Chili**

Ingredients
1 tablespoon olive oil
1 pound skinless boneless chicken breasts
6 cups water
4 cups chicken stock
½ cup tomato sauce
2 small onions, chopped
1 cup frozen corn
1 carrot and 1 stalk celery, sliced
1 big can diced tomatoes in juice
1 15-ounce can red kidney beans, drained
1 large jalapeno, seeded and diced
¼ cup chopped parsley
3 cloves garlic, minced
2 teaspoons chili powder
1 teaspoon cumin
1 teaspoon salt
dash of cayenne pepper, basil, and oregano

On the side:
1 cup grated cheddar cheese
½ cup sour cream
¼ cup finely chopped red onion
2 tablespoons chopped cilantro

Step 1

Make yourself a big vodka and cranberry juice with fresh lime. Heat olive oil in a large nonstick saucepan over medium-high heat. Sauté chicken on both sides for about 8 minutes per side. Remove from heat and cool until chicken can be handled. Do not wash pot.

Step 2

Shred the chicken and place back in pot with remaining ingredients and turn heat to high. Bring to a boil, then reduce heat and simmer covered for four hours. (Pace yourself on the cocktails during this dangerous waiting period.) Stir mixture frequently; chili will reduce substantially and darken.

Step 3

Refresh your drink and serve chili with grated cheddar, sour cream, chopped red onion, and cilantro.

Serves 4–6.

Take a look at the unintentionally hilarious exercise photos in pregnancy and baby magazines. The woman is always lying on pillows, looking like she's taking a nap, or doing something strenuous like raising her arms above her head. Hey, even I can do that! (Do not, by any means, skip ahead to the postpartum exercise sections of the magazines, where all you'll see are women with 2 percent body fat doing killer ab workouts. You'll have to wade in there soon enough.)

By all means, make a genuine effort to keep moving—and remember, walking is still the all-time best workout. Exercise makes you feel better, look better, and will keep your muscles healthy so you can deliver the Precious Bundle. Just don't expect your efforts to have much aesthetic effect. You're a soft body now.

For example, when I was about seven months along, a former lover of mine came to dinner. As he was saying goodbye, he reached around to give my backside an affectionate squeeze, a cheeky gesture that had unexpected consequences. Snatching his hand back like it had touched fire, he yelped and took two steps out of my personal space. "What the hell happened back there?" he asked crossly. Even though his rights to comment on the consistency of my butt had expired long ago, I still felt bad for him and apologized for his loss.

My advice? Don't let anybody who hasn't been a constant participant in your gradual softening go anywhere near your pillow parts. That would be your bottom, your thighs, your upper arms, and your bosom. And your brain, of course, but what man wants to go near that?

RULE #31:
Don't be prepared.

This is a corollary to Rule #10, "Don't take in stuff that scares you," but it's possibly even more important, because you are now—how can we put this delicately?—so completely unstable. About this time in your pregnancy, you're going to encounter a whole lot of freaky stuff. For instance, one book I picked up in my last month suggested that these final weeks before giving birth would be well spent contemplating how you would feel if your baby were born deformed. Another helpful resource suggested that by trying to calculate exactly how much pain you could stand, you'd be better prepared for the rigors of childbirth. I'm not sure how I was supposed to gauge my pain threshold, short of stabbing myself in the crotch, but the idea was presented as an eminently reasonable course of action. And for several brief and searing seconds, I did consider both suggestions. Then I chucked both books and went back to hunting for pictures of pregnant celebrities who were even fatter than I was.

Suffice to say, these troubling books/articles/people should be avoided at all costs. Right now, your mind and emotions are even more fragile than your stretched-tight-as-a-drum skin, so make a big effort to protect yourself, especially from those *Our Bodies, Ourselves* time travelers—women you barely know who are dying to share their gruesome labor stories with you. In detail. These stories will inevitably include all the E-words (episiotomy, epidural, eclampsia, etc.). My advice is to just smile brightly and say something like, "Gosh, I would love to hear how your vagina was cut from stem to stern, but my OB made me swear I wouldn't listen to a single labor story and ruin all the fun!" Then skedaddle away. You're entitled. You're pregnant. So there.

RULE #32:
Seize one last chance for irresponsibility.
Even though it may be more of a waddle, take a walk on the wild side. Drink your orange juice right out of the carton. Put your feet up on the table, where you can see them. Don't even think about doing laundry until you're down to your last pair of skivvies. (Okay, so I'm a tiny bit obsessive about housework and I didn't follow this last rule. But I would have, if only I'd known what was coming.)

It's important now to meet nobody's needs but your own. If you can't imagine what this would look like, observe your husband—or any male in the vicinity. Men have an incredible aptitude for meeting their own needs, and we could learn a lot from them if we weren't so concerned with how everybody else was "feeling." Unfortunately, I think most women are hardwired to take care of others, but that doesn't mean you can't do your level best to wrestle that old bugaboo to the ground during these last fleeting weeks of freedom. If you're an anal-retentive maniac like I am, and hence incapable of letting a domestic task slide without suffering severe mental anguish, confine yourself to personal acts of selfishness. Hog the pillows. Don't bring in the paper. Sleep in, if that's still possible. Wear socks to bed if you feel like it. Scratch whatever part of you itches. See? It really is liberating being a man.

RULE #33:

It's okay to be a puddle.

I hope I won't alienate anybody by saying this, but having a baby really puts you in touch with your animal side. Not your "I'm too sexy for my Volvo" animal side; your raw, primal, vulnerable, clawing, clutching animal side. Which makes perfect sense when you think about it. We were put here—in fact we *are* here—because we reproduce. It's what we're made to do. Babies *R* us! But like everything else in nature, when we reproduce, we are at our very weakest, most tender, and most in need of protection.

Speaking strictly for myself, this was not a place where I felt real comfy. In fact, I hated it—but that had a lot to do with the fact that I didn't have a mate I could lean on (or even find) and so I felt excruciatingly vulnerable. But even women with lovely, supportive mates can find it frightening to experience these huge tidal waves of fear, uncertainty, and primitive neediness.

All I can promise is that this, too, shall pass. You'll have your baby, and the sands will shift. You will be the one who's needed, not needy, and you will become the fierce protectoress. And as you slooooowly regain your figure and your kickass attitude, you might even find yourself missing the helpless drama of this time . . . at least for a minute or two. As an immediate remedy, I'd suggest my favorite nonalcoholic form of escapism—a movie—as long as it's not about a bad relationship or a woman at risk.

Following are ten of my personal favorites.

Top Ten Feel-Good Movies for Knocked-Up Gals

Sound of Music—Mystery mother has seven kids, then dies, but tuneful nanny inspires and loves them all, then takes on both stepmom role and the Nazis.

My Fair Lady—Uber-waif Audrey Hepburn will make you feel like a whale, but she becomes inexplicably attracted to pompous ass Rex Harrison, so it's a happy ending.

Parenthood—Recovering alcoholic patriarch, loser brother, bonehead boss, stressed-out dad and underachieving kids—if it weren't funny it would be almost too much like real life.

What About Bob?—Hyperneurotic obsessive-compulsive freak Bill Murray stalks his new shrink Richard Dreyfuss, driving him to murderous paranoid rage. (It's a *comedy*, folks.)

When Harry Met Sally—Meg Ryan and Billy Crystal suffer through each other's crass youth and bad relationships, develop a great friend-ship, then ruin it by having sex. (Been there . . . .)

Tootsie—Difficult, washed-up actor Dustin Hoffman wants the starring role in a soap so much, he sinks to becoming a woman to get it, then finds he's a better man for the sex change.

Moonstruck—Unlikely spinster Cher smacks around a besotted young Nicolas Cage while a resplendent, neglected Olympia Dukakis flirts with infidelity. Pasta lust galore.

Groundhog Day—Every day, an unrepentant Bill Murray wakes up to the exact same stupid day—great preparation for your life after baby.

Sleepless in Seattle—Sweet little morsel with a great soundtrack in a shameless takeoff on *An Affair to Remember*, sans wheelchair (which is sorta cheating).

Fargo—Very pregnant Frances McDormand solves botched kidnapping/murder plot while taking on frightening restaurant buffets and thick Minnesota accents. Enjoy!

RULE #34:
Hold out for Baby's Dr. Right.

This is the fun part, because it signifies that you're actually going to have a baby who needs a doctor, not just a big fat stomach that needs an OB. Thanks to Mr. Wrong's reproductive network, I also found the best pediatrician on the planet: Dr. Dean, a gorgeous Rupert Everett look-alike who was incredibly supportive, kind, responsive, informative, compassionate, and complimentary, never failing to tell me what a great job I was doing. Plus, Dr. Dean gave great literature. This is important because your office visits with the baby are sure to be jammed full of information shared, shots given, tears dried, and anxieties dispersed. So you're going to want to have something to look back upon at home that answers the questions you forgot to ask and reiterates the critical details, which have now escaped you, along with your baby's pacifier and adorable hat. Every visit, Dr. Dean would write all of Lulu's vital statistics on a three-page handout that went into great detail about just what should be happening at that stage of the baby's life. It was indispensable. My current pediatrician, although very nice, offers nothing of the sort, and I feel a bit lost without it. I loved knowing how long Lulu should be sleeping, what her eating habits should be, what parameters she fell into in terms of height and weight, and which behavioral and learning cues to look for. (And because the days when your child will predictably do anything he or she is supposed to are numbered, I would strongly urge you to take full advantage of this fleeting parental thrill.)

When you're evaluating a pediatrician, talk to other parents and ask about speed of callback if your child is sick, whether you'll see the same doctor all the time (a huge advantage), and overall comfort and satisfaction. Then go interview the doctor and let your instincts guide you. You're going to be talking to your pediatrician quite a bit, even if your baby is perfectly healthy. Choose someone you like talking to.

RULE #35:
Stop being The Nice Patient.
Many women, in an attempt to be "nice," make the mistake of hesitating to burden their obstetrician with "petty" concerns. Please. Burden away. Don't be afraid to ask questions. Your body is going through an enormous transformation and it's okay to feel flustered about it. Information is the best antidote to panic, so confront your worries/anxieties/doubts and get them answered. If you're the independent type, go to books or pregnancy Web sites. But personal attention is often what you really need. When it comes to your time with the doc, do *not* mistake timidity for politeness. An average birth in this country will net the obstetrician a hefty bundle. Get your money's worth.

angela acts out
When I had my first baby, I had a c-section. So when I was going to have my second, my OB really wanted me to try a VBAC. But I was totally not into it. I figure: you lose a few stomach muscles, okay, they come back. But your vagina you pretty much need for the rest

of your life. I was a lot more scared of an episiotomy or a great rip-ping tear than I was of a c-section. My OB didn't really approve of my choice, but guess what? He wasn't having the baby.

RULE #36:
Quench the home fires.

I never understood the concept of heartburn until my eighth month of pregnancy, when I lay down after a meal and was convinced someone had just poured lighter fluid down my trachea. I'm not a big proponent of drugs (that's what my col-lege years were for), so I decided to take another route, which you might also like to follow. Chances are, in these final days you're not going to be able to handle much in terms of quan-tity of food, so compensate for that in sheer quality. Make sure everything you eat is rather bland, small, expensive, and horri-bly indulgent. Go to one of those fabulously overpriced whole foods places and load up on organic and lovingly prepared deli-cacies that will satiate you right to the quivering edge of guilt. Avoid anything with tomatoes or a high citrus quotient, as well as anything sinfully rich. Serve your delicacies on your prettiest plates. Then just hope they don't come back to haunt you.

RULE #37:
Play up your knees.

Turn sideways, turn backward, turn upside down. You're still going to look like a beach ball. There is very little you can do about this situation, except deliver. In the meantime, if ever there were a time for snazzy accessories, this is it. Anything to tear attention away from that swollen center of attraction: your stomach. Don't bother to buy new shoes; your feet are probably going to swell up like balloons and you won't be able to see them anyhow. (Not to mention the horror of having some poor shoe-store clerk kneel between your knees and attempt to jam your chubby tootsies into a pump.) Now is the time to spring for some buttery-smooth leather gloves, gorgeous scarves, and colorful tights. If it's summer and you can't bear the thought of anything touching your flesh, buy some beautiful hair bands, bandanas, and scrunchies to tie up your hair. Dramatic earrings are a brilliant distraction. New lipstick is always highly recommended. And since your neck is not likely to be a big trouble spot, a couple of dazzling new necklaces are definitely in order. Shop on.

Bonus Pointer for Space Moms:
Get driven.

When you're roughly the size of Rhode Island, the small tasks of life can become rather daunting. It's time to ask for help from anyone who has the bad sense to stay in the same room as you. Some women stop working during the last few weeks in order to relax, prepare the baby's room, or simply to prevent serial office maiming. I was more afraid of the psychotic decorating damage I would do at home, so I worked until the bitter end.

Coworkers were begging me to quit, but I courageously plowed them over. However, I did enlist their help in scratching my stomach (just kidding) and in helping me remember where I left things.

Yes, due to the hormonal bath you're now immersed in, your memory, like mine, may slip into a slowdown or complete work stoppage. I lost my purse every single day. I could never remember where I parked my car. Speaking automotively, you may also lose the ability to drive well—or even legally. I'm astonished I didn't completely total my car while pregnant, because I would routinely space out mid-freeway debating whether James or Julian was the preferable moniker, and only regain consciousness as I pulled into the parking garage and proceeded to park the car through the depths of another progesterone fog. If at all possible, get someone else to dress you, drive you, park your car, and place your handbag somewhere highly visible. You've got better things to do. You're pregnant.

CHAPTER FOUR

Labor Rules: The Big Day(s)

getting there is half the fun

I suspect that every labor is absolutely unique. There's little use in me telling you about mine when yours is sure to be utterly different. But though it may not be terribly helpful, my Eleven Tales of Labor may prove mildly entertaining/somewhat revolting/potentially illuminating—if only because when you hit a hard spot, you'll know it's just par for the course, to use a totally inappropriate golfing analogy. (And yes, I do realize I have now slipped into the realms of those "Let me tell you about my 850 hours of labor" wretches that I warned you to avoid. Oh well.)

RULE #38:
Pack light.

In retrospect, the whole concept of packing for the hospital is a bit ridiculous. If you have a normal birth, they're going to

61

Jolene's Labor Concierge List

Betty may counsel you to pack light, but I say take everything that will make you feel fabulous in your most pressing hour of need.

My suggestions:

Chanel No. 5

Aveda love lotion

Nail polish

Makeup, especially lipstick, for photos after the birth, when you'll look spectral

Lovely hankies—not for the baby, nudnik, but for your glistening brow!

Stone water fountains

A tape of sacred temple sounds

Your favorite James Brown CD

A fabulous kimono to wear around the hospital afterward

Your entire collection of Chippendales posters

discharge you before you have time to use a toothbrush, much less require a change of clothing. And if you have a c-section, they're going to keep you in that hospital gown for days, tromping up and down the halls until you "pass wind" and become accustomed to walking with stitches in your nether regions. As for the baby's couture, the hospital swaddling clothes are so cute and precious, you don't really need anything but the baby's revered "home from the hospital" outfit. So I wouldn't go overboard on the overnight bag. Having said that, I confess that I probably packed my bag seven or eight times, if for no other reason than it was a comforting reminder that I was eventually going to have a baby and wasn't going to be pregnant for another fifteen years or so. The only thing I forgot was my toothbrush, which I did, in fact, need because I did, in fact, have the c-section I was definitely not going to have.

RULE #39:
Don't tempt fate.

Some of my best friends have delivered their babies at home, with absolutely no problem. And I still think you have to be completely out of your mind to take that chance. (See? I really don't have to be politically correct here.) Because in addition to those lucky women, I've also had several friends who ended up having really scary, life-and-death type deliveries in which the baby needed to be rushed into ICU, and the new mothers almost bled to death. Unless you have a burning desire to relive those days of yesteryear when women—and babies, let's not forget—routinely died during childbirth, I don't know why you'd risk your one big opportunity to have a healthy birth just so you can stay at home and be natural. Eat a granola bar—and go to the hospital.

Bevan's home rule

Betty was born politically incorrect, but I think I must interject here and tell you that I think the fear-mongering Rule above is really Not On (as we like to politely say in England). I firmly believe that home births are a wonderful idea so long as you have a qualified, experienced midwife at your side. For one thing, women have been happily having their babies at home for a millennium or two, so it's actually not the recklesss, madcap idea that a lot of hospitals would like you to believe. Second, your chances of having a natural childbirth and avoiding a c-section are increased exponentially at home, since as we all know, hospitals are in the business of giving drugs and performing surgeries, and they will always err on the side of caution (or the expeditious choice). Finally, women as a rule take responsibility for everything unfortunate that happens in their children's lives, whether or not anybody could have done anything to prevent it . . . and I want to go on record here as encouraging us all to just bloody stop doing that! Thank you, and have a lovely baby.

RULE #40:
Pretty up.

Not that it's going to make one smidge of difference in how you get through labor, but you might want to consider getting a nice pedicure and keeping your legs shaved so you don't find yourself worried about whether the hunky resident who's watching your epidural is going to be grossed out by your personal hygiene. To be brutally honest, if you do have the epidural, you will essentially lose all feeling in the lower half of your body, which will give you the vivid, if completely inaccurate, impression that you're invisible from the waist down. An oddly comforting sensation when it seems like half the male staff of the hospital is trotting in to look at your vagina. But as long as your toes look pretty and your legs are smooth, who cares, right?

RULE #41:
Use your voice.

When I finally went into labor, it didn't feel anything like I expected. I wasn't even sure I was having contractions. I just felt weird. Of course, they tell you not to eat. (As if when every part of your female anatomy goes into hellzapoppin' overdrive, you're likely to slam down a ham sandwich?) I just kept feeling weirder and weirder, like something enormous was happening inside, but nothing felt specific—no pain, no physical signs of anything.

Then waves of cramping started in earnest, and at 2 A.M. I told Mr. Wrong to stay at my house with his daughter, called my labor coach Bevan, and headed for the hospital. They examined me and determined I was in pre-labor, told me to just lie in bed or walk around, and promised that the doctor would be in about 7 A.M. Bevan was exhausted from having worked at the restaurant all night, and once we got into the labor waiting room, she asked me if it was okay if she just lay down for a bit. Even though the pain was getting more and more intense, to the point of scaring me silly, I said "Sure, why should both of us be up all night?" and went into the bathroom and started throwing up.

Four hours later, I was still throwing up, but now I was in serious agony. These were like the worst cramps of my life, multiplied by a thousand. The only relief from the ridiculous amount of pain I was feeling came from lying on the floor of the shower and letting fiery hot water beat down on me. Lulu had apparently flipped over to nestle comfortably against my spine, so I was experiencing all the joys of back labor. I was miserable, scared, and feeling enormously sorry for myself. I guess maybe I should have taken that "Pain Threshold Quiz," because mine was turning out to be shamefully low. The idea that you could breathe through the pain seemed preposterous. I was even trying to cry quietly, because I didn't want to wake up Bevan—which brings me to my next suggestion. Don't ever think this is the time to be selfless and not cause a ruckus. This is Big Fuss Time, and don't you forget it. Wake up your birth partner if he or she is wimping out on you. Wake up the whole ward if you feel like it. You don't get any points for going through labor with quiet stoicism—or if you do, you don't want them. Grab help with both hands, by the lapels, and make somebody give you the companionship, the ice chips, the back massage, or whatever it is you need. And P.S.: It's a proven fact that hollering when it hurts helps you work through the pain, so don't hold back.

RULE #42:
Consider the midwife/doula option.
For some reason (Narrow-mindedness? Stupidity? Both?) I hadn't wanted to work with a midwife or a doula. I guess I had this feeling that I would get saddled with some motherly woman who would just want to talk, talk, talk throughout my two efficient hours of labor, trying to get me to breathe, and holding out on the drugs. As it turned out, all I wanted when I was in labor was some motherly woman who would talk,

talk, talk to me and convince me I wasn't dying—and not hold out on the drugs.

Let's be candid here. Labor, in my case, was a long, bewildering, scary trip to hell. And not even your closest friend or devoted mate is going to necessarily want, or know how, to accompany you on that journey. It's really something that you should entrust to a professional. (News Flash: This is not your OB. Your OB is there for the big push, but he or she is certainly not going to be there holding your hand during the endless hours of moaning and groaning. Nor are your overworked and underpaid OB nurses.) The only one who's going to do that, who's going to *want* to do that, is a doula. Or possibly your helpful mate—but see the next Rule on the potential problems inherent in that. Now I don't know what kind of labor you will have—and more significantly, neither do you. So it's important that you're covered for all eventualities. And in retrospect, I really wish I had signed up for the Doula Special. (In a hospital, some midwives may not stay with you during your entire labor.) Of course, doulas do cost money, and be forewarned, most health plans won't cover that expense. But I think it's probably a small price to pay for your sanity during labor.

RULE #43:
Re: The helpful mate.

I didn't have one, so I can't speak in the first person about this. But I know what I've been told—and it's not terribly encouraging. My friend Herb, who is about as decent and sweet as a man can be, was thrilled to be with Beth at the birth of their daughter. He rubbed Beth's back, helped her breathe, and was trying to feed her some ice chips when suddenly, out of nowhere, she snarled, "Get away from me. I can't even stand the sight of you. Get out of here right this minute!" (You'd have to know Beth to understand what a completely demonic departure this represents from her usual unflappable and patient self.) So Herb, feeling a bit rejected, went to the far corner of the room, picked up a magazine, and started to read. At which point Beth caught a glimpse of him engrossed in *Travel & Leisure* while she was suffering through the most excruciating pain of her life—pain caused directly by the penis of THAT MAN SITTING THERE READING A TRAVEL MAGAZINE—and she just flipped out. "Are you READING while I'm in LABOR? Are you actually sitting there READING about VACATIONS while I'm having a BABY???" To this day, Herb still has trouble picking up a magazine without first looking around to see who might attack.

I think it must be hard for guys to go through labor. They know that their penises caused all this suffering (and subsequent joy) and there's nothing they can do about it, short of standing there sheepishly telling you to breathe. It must be scary, too, to see all that pain and not be able to alleviate it. Perhaps there are some men who are so highly evolved that they're able to function as knowledgeable and deeply caring labor coaches, but I sorta doubt it. In fact, I think it's far more likely that you're really going to want to clobber a know-it-all guy like that when you're looking down the barrel of an episiotomy. But that's just me.

RULE #44:
Relieve yourself.

When my OB finally arrived at 7 A.M., I was pretty sure I was right on the verge of transition. In fact, I was convinced he was going to look up in surprise at my terrific, if lonely, progress and say those magic words: "Okay, Betty, it's time to push." Instead he told a sleepy Bevan she could go back to bed, then asked me if I wanted to go home to wait it out because I wasn't dilated at all. Fully effaced. Not one stinking centimeter dilated. You mean it was going to get worse? My OB must have remembered I was about ten days past my due date when I grabbed him by the stethoscope and whispered, "Home? You can't send me home. I HAVE NO HOME!" He assured me I was doing fine, I just had a little back labor going on because my baby was turned the wrong way, but yes, I was definitely going to have my baby that day, come hell or high water, ha ha ha. Then he proceeded to break my water (ha ha ha, these OBs are such wits) and put me on Pitocin to hurry things along. I wasn't about to hurry anything along when I already felt like I was about to deliver my own spine, so when he asked me if I wanted "pain relief," I readily agreed. The epidural man came in and did his thing, and Bevan slept on. Of course, now her snoring seemed sort of cute, since I could no longer feel anything south of my sternum.

At this point, I started watching TV. Yes, through the miracle of modern pharmacology, I had been transformed from a piteous, whimpering wretch on the shower floor to a . . . sports fan. I watched golf. Then basketball. Then tennis. (Apparently, the TV was programmed for the pain relief of dads, because all I could find to watch was a full selection of sports channels.)

Pretty soon Mr. Wrong showed up, then ran off to complete some errands because my progress had slowed to nothing. Then my OB came in and freaked out. I thought the little machine measuring my contractions had been jumping around a bit, but how was I to know? Apparently, I was having "titanic" contractions due to the Pitocin, so now I needed a muscle relaxant to calm my uterus down. Okay. Then it was back on the Pitocin, and back to tennis. Mr. Wrong returned, and Bevan ran home to check on her kids. After having briefly achieved 1.5 centimeters' dilation, I was now moving backward. The epidural was still working, so I wasn't in pain, but the total lack of progress was getting discouraging and I was becoming deeply weary of ESPN.

At 4 P.M., the OB told me he thought I was going to need a c-section. He used the square-peg-in-a-round-hole analogy. He said the baby's head was starting to get a little swollen from all that banging into my not-one-bit dilated cervix. I could not believe what I was hearing. How was I going to bond with my baby and hold it on my tummy and establish that critically important mother/baby connection if I had a cesarean? I decided to try one more hour.

At 5 P.M., I was 1 cm dilated. And my OB said the magic words: "If you get the c-section, you'll see your baby in five minutes."

RULE #45:
Don't look back (as I will now do).

When I think back on my labor, I really do wonder what would have happened if I hadn't gone on the Pitocin, hadn't had the epidural, and had employed a more active labor coach. (No offense meant to Bevan: I just should never have expected her to act as my midwife simply because she is so enormously entertaining.) Sure, somebody might have ended up with a chair embedded in his or her forehead—or I might have had a vaginal birth. I don't think I'm one of those women who would have died in childbirth on the prairie in days of yore, but I could be wrong about that. In any event, your chances of having a normal birth will be significantly increased if you can hold off on the drugs and at least give your body the chance to do what it's trying to do. (Then again, one forgets about the pain—and it was simply ghastly. I just cannot believe somebody could breathe through that. Not through back labor.) However, now that I'm safely on the far side of the labor dispute, I believe you should save any regrets you may feel about the delivery for all the huge things you're going to do to screw up your Precious Bundle henceforward. Look, even if you didn't have the birthing experience you wanted, you still got the baby you adore. And birth is as good a time as any to start getting used to the fact that you are no longer in exclusive control of your life. (Gulp!)

naomi's rule of self-preservation

It never occurred to me *not* to have pain relief. I've been a vegetarian forever and spent my formative years (what I can remember of them) in Boulder, so I believe in natural everything. Except childbirth. When you're pregnant, you agonize over what's "right" to do, and I felt a lot of pressure not to "drug" my baby—but I also wanted not to "chew" my husband's arm off in the delivery room. And the whole argument for a natural birth just didn't make sense to me. The baby is going to get smashed like a grape going through the birth canal, then shoved out into a completely foreign, noisy, and bright environment. That's not exactly a calming experience, no matter how you look at it. Anyway, I truly believe it's not a big deal either way. The baby's the prize, not the way it gets here.

RULE #46:
Say "Hello, beautiful."

The c-section itself wasn't so bad. Really. You have plenty of pain relief—to such a point that you can't feel anything below the sheet they stretch across your chest to prevent you from passing out at the sight of what they're doing down there. A lot of people crowd around, performing what feels like a tire change on your abdomen. And then, amazingly, astonishingly, abruptly, they pull a gorgeous, perfect, lovely baby out of your stomach. After all that time, I still could not believe there was a baby in there! And how did he get so pink and pearly in all that darkness?

"You have a beautiful baby girl," my OB crowed. And I was so sure I was having a boy. But a girl! Perfect! Just exactly what I wanted! She yelped and hollered when they put her on the table and started to clean her off; then Mr. Right-for-Once picked her up and brought her over to me so I could see her. And together we looked for the first time into the beautiful, perfect, sweet, darling face of our baby. That was, and still remains, the most miraculous, most fabulous day of my life.

mary lou's darling birthing story

I've had four girls, all with natural labor. [Betty aside: *Yes, she is one of those Pez dispensers I was telling you about.*] With my last girl, Christy, I went into the hospital and I guess everybody figured I was such an old pro at this birthing business, they didn't have much to worry much about. The Olympics were on and my husband and doctor were engrossed in watching the TV. I was having a really hard time, so when I heard the nurse enter the room, I was relieved and thankful to have a woman in there with me. She came over to the bed, held my hand, and stroked it softly as she murmured, "Oh, she is darling. Isn't she just so sweet?" I couldn't believe she was talking about me, huge and lumpy in the throes of an eyes-squeezed-shut contraction, but I was grateful for her attempt to cheer me up. She thought I was sweet! I looked up in gratitude, only to see her eyes above her mask, gazing in unblinking admiration at Kristi Yamaguchi pirouetting around the ice rink on TV. "Hey! I'm having a BABY here!" I hollered. That woke 'em up.

RULE #47:
Prep for Post-op.

The aftermath of a c-section can be pretty harsh, so just beware. I started throwing up, shaking like a leaf, got freezing cold, and couldn't stop vibrating for a solid hour. Basically, you go from being ecstatic to going seriously into shock. But then you come out of it and can't wait to see your darling little pal again.

I got wheeled back to my private room—pale, dazed, drugged, and looking hideous—only to run into my Lamaze coach and her new class on their walk-through room tour. Fourteen couples stared at me in horrified disbelief. With my matted hair, bleary eyes, drug-swollen face and IV tube taped to my arm, I was not exactly a poster child for natural childbirth.

"How'd it go?" my Lamaze coach unwisely asked.

"Great!" I croaked from the gurney. "Fifteen hours of labor. Major drugs. And a c-section."

You've never seen twenty-nine people scatter so fast.

"Don't forget to breathe!" I yelped after them.

If it weren't for my staples, I'd have been in stitches.

RULE #48:
Celebrate the Birth Day.

As far as I'm concerned, every birth is a sacred moment.

It's the closest we get to God on this earth.

Revel in it.

And say a prayer of thanksgiving to whatever Higher Being you choose.

Weird OB Fact

Most OBs are almost entirely focused on you, the mommy, and are not actually baby-lovers at all. In fact, once the baby is safely delivered, you may have some trouble keeping the doctor's attention. A few days after Lulu was born, Dr. Reid visited me in the hospital and I urged, "The baby's so healthy and cute! Did you look at her? She's right over there in the bassinet!" Never looking up from my abdomen, Reid crowed, "God, that is the smallest incision ever—you're not going to be able to see that scar at all!" And he bounced out of the room with nary a backward glance at the product of all his hard work. Never mind. That's what pediatricians are for.

Bonus Pointer for Controlling Moms:
Straight from the nurse's mouth.

My Pilates teacher, Leigh, is gorgeous, effervescent, *and* delivers babies for a living. Personally, I can't imagine anyone better to have by your side when you're having a baby (or trying to do a decent roll-up), but unless you live in Philly, you're not going to have the luxury of laboring with Nurse Leigh. So I'm bringing her to you *in absentia*. Listen up, y'all.

From all the deliveries I've seen, I think the stronger a mother's need for control, the more issues she's likely to encounter during labor. The women who seem to have the best deliveries come in with an open mind and a laid-back attitude. I know it's hard to get to that mellow place because a lot of books tell you that you should go into the hospital with a definitive game plan for your labor—but that's a bit like having a definitive game plan for boating down the Amazon. You have no idea what wild things await you out there! And when you are super-attached to doing your labor in a specific way, it can be hard for you to cope when the unexpected happens—which in the delivery room is what we're always expecting.

I try to gently suggest that if you can leave your pre-conceived notions behind, you'll be able to get through the process . . . well, not necessarily more easily . . . but more happily. If you're convinced that an epidural means you're a failure, then when the pain gets really bad and you want one, you're going to feel awful. That's just pointless. About 70 to 80 percent of our patients end up requesting pain relief, and there's no shame in that. Or some women have their hearts set on breastfeeding immediately after the baby is born because they've heard it helps you bond with your child. But quite a few babies have trouble breathing right after delivery, and they need medical attention, not a breast. Why disappoint yourself or stress over the little things in labor and delivery, when the big joy is the baby's arrival? Let it go!

The whole idea that there is one right way to have a baby is sort of funny. A lot of women tell me they feel like bad mothers if they don't want to have natural childbirth or don't want to keep their babies in their rooms. Invariably, these are highly successful, confident women who would normally kick your butt if you tried to boss them into so much as a vinaigrette. But when it comes to having a baby, some of these same uber-achievers become totally insecure and unsure of themselves. Check your backbones, ladies! This is *your* baby, and you get to have it any way you want. The only important thing in labor is that the baby is delivered safe and healthy and whole. And however that happens, your delivery is a success.

One thing I always try to warn people about: With the nursing shortage and all the pressures of the delivery room, you are not going to have your nurse's uninterrupted attention during the entire duration of your labor. I usually have two or three patients in labor at a time, and I have to constantly check vital signs, update charts, and run from room to room. If you want someone to be your labor coach and sit by your bed through the whole thing, you really need a doula. Your nurse simply won't have the time to breathe through fifteen hours of contractions with you (and she'll go off shift, anyhow). I just hate to disappoint people who come in expecting that level of attention when I'm physically not able to provide it.

Oh, and a special note for dads: Please don't ask your delivery nurse to explain the engineering mechanics of the fetal monitor to you when she's busy checking your wife's vital signs. It's very distracting and let's face it, if you really wanted to know, you'd probably have gone to nursing school.

Happy delivery!

CHAPTER FIVE

Mother Rules: 0 to 3 Months— The Precious Bundle

out of the frying pan . . .

O kay, so now that all the waiting is over and your own Precious Bundle has actually arrived . . . what the hell are you supposed to do next? This is virgin territory, so to speak. On the one hand, you have dozens of reasons to have a total nervous breakdown: Postpartum mood swings, swollen, leaky breasts, lack of sleep, raging insecurity that you have no business at all being entrusted with an infant. On the other hand, you have this immense, astonishing flood of love for the little baby in the bassinet right next to your bed. That sweet little face. Those darling hands. That satiny skin. For me, it was no contest. I was ecstatically happy—despite the fact that my outer world had pretty much fallen apart.

During week two of Lulu's life, Mr. Wrong took me out to the movies. Instead of going into the theater, we sat in the parking lot watching the sun set behind the Rocky Mountains and talking. Then he popped the question. Would I mind if he started dating again? He explained that he was probably not going to be around much in the future. And that weekend, he took this Other Daughter and his Other Girlfriend up to Aspen, and Lulu and I didn't see him again for about three months.

That is not a great beginning for a baby's life. But somehow, it was. It was summer. It was beautiful in Colorado. I wasn't working, which *was* fabulous in and of itself. And I had the perfect baby. Every morning I would wake up to her gorgeous, happy face—huge blue eyes in a darling round face—and my heart would leap for joy. She slept straight through the night from almost the first week. She had a great appetite, was a highly competent and considerate nurser, and she remained healthy as a filly. She was alert and active and completely captivating. And she was a good traveler.

Before you decide you hate me for having such good luck, consider this. She had to be. I was an emotional wreck and definitely without the resilience for coping with any nonsense like colic, and she knew that. So she made it easy for me. (Of course, she's paying me back now, but that's okay. I'm up for it.)

But let's be honest: The first months can be hard even if Daddy isn't dating. And some women do get overwhelmed with the sheer weight of all that newborn neediness. Just try not to let the hardness steal anything from the sweetness. This is your time to fall madly in love, to lie in bed for hours admiring every inch of that tiny body, to stare into those newly opened eyes and see the gorgeous creature you brought into this world, who you're going to know forever—your time to kiss and hug and cuddle and coo and sing and rock and nuzzle.

In short, this time is a stupendous treasure. These Fifteen Righteous Rules will help you rock your first months of motherhood.

RULE #49:
Enjoy the stay.

After giving birth, some women can't wait to get out of the hospital. My friend Shan was home eating pizza four hours after she gave birth to Daniel. My friend Bevan never went to the hospital at all and had both her babies at home. (But who cleaned up afterward? It haunts me.) Being shallow, I was deliriously happy that I'd had a c-section, if only because that meant I could stay in the hospital longer. I would have gladly stayed for weeks. I loved the morphine drip. I loved the call button. I loved the way you could buzz and ask them to bring your baby in, please. Most of all, I loved the hospital at night when everything was quiet and the nurses were chatting softly and you could roam the halls, padding down to the nursery to watch your baby sleep, then dreamily padding back to your room filled with flowers and fall asleep yourself. I found the hospital utterly relaxing and infinitely soothing. Like a cocoon.

My advice is to stay as long as they'll let you.

maggie's LA sister's rule

My sister lives in LA, so she's a little neurotic about her weight. Like, if she weighs anything, it's a crisis. Needless to say, she spent her entire pregnancy on the treadmill and in the pool, trying not to gain a pound more than she was absolutely required to—in total pregnancy denial. Her labor was really hard and they had to take her into surgery. When she woke up, the first thing she saw was the IV she was hooked up to and she totally freaked.

"Oh my God!" she shrieked, "what's going on here?"

"Don't worry, " I assured her, "your baby's *fine.*"

Still fixated on the IV, she demanded, "Exactly how many calories have they been pumping into me since I've been unconscious?"

And you thought you were shallow.

RULE #50:

Go home with everything.

If your hospital is anything like mine, you're in for a boatload of freebies. Help yourself! Seriously, take the formula. Take the diapers. Take the little cotton crib liners. Take the booties and caps and onesies, the laundry soap, the Tylenol, the washcloths, and did I mention the diapers? You'll save yourself a pile of cash, you'll have stuff on hand when you really need it, and you'll get something for the $18,000 a day the hospital is charging. And lest you think this constitutes pilfering, get a grip. Companies like Johnson & Johnson love to give stuff away at the hospitals, because they're hoping to make you a loyal Huggies mommy right from birth.

Who cares what their motives are? Just take the stuff and run. Especially if they're giving away those sweet little hooded towels. These things are totally cute, eminently practical, and soft as a baby's bottom. For some reason, a freshly washed baby smells even more delicious when he's all bundled up like a terry-cloth ice cream cone.

These towels work well even into toddlerhood, since kids can run around after their bath, hoods on their heads, pretending to be Batman, Wonder Woman, or Mick Jagger. Very cool.

RULE #51:
Nobody Is ready to be a mother.

Enough beating around the bush. Sooner or later, they're going to let you out of the hospital with your baby. This is a mind-blowing experience. Here are hundreds of people with fancy medical degrees and oodles of professional expertise, letting you walk out of the hospital in sole possession of a baby you met just a few days ago. In a surreal progression of events, they kick you out of your comfortable room, take your money, discharge you, and set you out on the sidewalk, babe in arms. Then you go home, put the baby in the bassinet, and try to act normal. All afternoon, I kept looking at Lulu, she kept looking back at me, and honestly, it was as if we were both waiting for the knock on the door: "Okay, the game's over. Give the baby back and let's bring this little caper to an end."

But the only knock on the door was from Bevan, inviting me to dinner next door. That was so nice! She had made her famous Pasta Diablo. *Diablo* means Satan. A few words to the wise: Do not eat anything bearing the words "caliente," "devil," or "diablo" on the first night home from the hospital. My calm little Lulu, after a few gulps of breastmilk diablo, went ballistic. She screamed and hollered from 9 P.M. until well after midnight. I was crying, she was sobbing; it was a totally pathetic scene. We finally fell asleep, damp with tears, tangled up together on the bed at about 2 A.M. . . . and awoke the next morning, sunshine streaming across the bed, to a brand-new day. She was still breathing! I hadn't killed her yet!

Little victories—such as living through the night—mean a lot.

Take things slowly. Breathe deeply and tell yourself everybody starts out this way. It's true. Plus, you're the only mother your baby's ever had, so how will she know that you're an utter novice? You can learn to do this together. Remember to breathe. Remember to have a glass of wine. Remember to tell yourself what a great job you're doing.

nina's sleep deprivation rule

The first few weeks of Freya's life, I was hanging in there. Then, quite abruptly, the lack of sleep caught up with me and for the next four months, I had no more than four hours of sleep a night. I went into this endless, gray, half-awake, zombie zone. Weeping all the time, I found myself wondering why in hell I ever took this on, and convincing myself that by becoming a mother I had totally ruined my life, which was obviously not the case. Just remember, the darkest hour is just before dawn. And I should know, because I was up for every one of those bloody sunrises. What nobody ever told me is that precisely when you hit the wall and think you can't possibly get through another minute and will simply have to return the baby for a full refund and try it again some other time—right after that, it all gets better. Almost magically. You get a bit of sleep, you wake up feeling refreshed, and everything looks possible.

Honestly, I've been through it twice now and that's what happens.

RULE #52:
Hold on tight.

Baby's first bath is another one of mommy's new hurdles. Sure, they show you how to do it in the hospital with a plastic doll. It's a tiny bit more challenging with a squirmy, satiny, breakable baby who is bound and determined to slip through your fingers. How the hell are you supposed to hold her *and* wash her? One hand is supporting the baby's head, the other is clutching her little body, your giant breasts are getting in the way of everything—the possibilities for disaster are endless. (Unless, of course, you get in the bathtub with her, in which case, it's immensely simple.) What you really need is a Velcro flap on your baby's back, but unfortunately, evolution hasn't seen to that yet. Which is why God invented mothers and mothers-in-law.

RULE #53:
Find some helping hands.

It's a fine old tradition. You have a baby, and your mother or mother-in-law comes to help out for a week or so. Why, then, does this so often lead to homicidal feelings and permanent frissons of resentment? I wouldn't know. My mom had passed away years before Lulu arrived and Mr. Wrong's mom was . . . well, Mrs. Wrong. Duhhhhhh. So my sister stepped in. And Kathy was brilliant. She took a week off work and schlepped all the way across country to offer me her cool, calm collectedness. She made me meals. She admired Lulu. She helped me get my breast pump and gave Lulu her first bath. She took me shopping for nursing bras and nightgowns. In short, she gave me exactly what I needed: confidence, good company, a lot of help, and a lucid evaluation of the odds that Mr. Wrong would hang around (that would be zero). I'd rent Kathy out for every new mom, but unfortunately, she's busy saving the leatherback turtles in St. Croix. Sorry.

gabrielle's worst-case scenario

My mother-in-law came out to help, right after Aaron was born. Everybody else thought that was so nice; I thought I would lose my mind. Whenever I put Aaron down, she picked him up. If I thought he was hungry, she thought he was tired. If I said he needed to burp, she said he needed to poop. I was exhausted and she took advantage of my weakness to prove that she knew more than me. So what? He was *my* baby. But I felt like I was competing with her for my baby's affection and my position as his mother. It all culminated one night when my in-laws took my husband and me out to dinner as a special treat. It was summer, we were dining outdoors, and my mother-in-law was convinced the baby was freezing to death. Before we even made it through appetizers, we had literally wrestled a blanket on and off him seven times. She just couldn't stand to let me make even the smallest decision about the baby. Finally, I got so mad, I made my husband leave the restaurant without us even eating. My in-laws left the next day and we didn't speak for months. It was total insanity. But I was still right!

RULE #54:
Milk it.

My mother, milk provider for every one of us eight children, was a volunteer for La Leche League. She protested tirelessly against Nestlé for encouraging poor mothers in Third-World countries to buy its formula instead of breastfeeding. She was an ardent believer in the benefits of nursing and could expound on them at length. In short, in our family, breastfeeding was bred in the bone. And I loved it! I couldn't get over the idea that you could simply take your baby and go, having everything you needed to feed her right in your own body. How cool is that?

To pick up my mother's baton and carry the flag for breastfeeding, I'm going to give you a few tips about nursing that nobody ever gave me.

First, let somebody help you the first couple of times—whether it's your mom, a La Leche volunteer, a lactation expert, or your midwife. I was still in the hospital when my milk came in, because I'd had the great good sense to get a c-section. A hospital breastfeeding consultant came to my room and instructed me in the latching-on and imparted a dozen other helpful tips. She was so helpful and encouraging, I felt enormously more confident and relaxed about nursing—which is really half the battle. Breastfeeding is not something you can simply read about online; this is one of those times when having a real person there to guide you really helps. And if the lactation consultant you've chosen isn't being helpful and positive, or is telling you that you don't have enough milk or you're

The Milky Way

If you weren't lucky enough to have a caesarean, and thus don't get to stay in the hospital till the cows come home (so to speak), you can get breastfeeding support from:

The International Lactation Consultant Association
919-787-5181; www.ilca.org

La Leche League International
800-525-3243 or 847-519-7730; www.lalecheleague.org

Other good Web sites include:
www.breastfeeding.com
www.4woman.gov/breastfeeding
www.webmd.com

not going to be able to breastfeed, get a second opinion. Get a second pediatrician. Just don't give up. Honestly, this is the way our species survived, for godsakes, so it really can't be that inefficient. You can do it!

Second, get the turbo pump. When your milk first comes in, your breasts can become mountainous. Hard. Incredibly painful. Frighteningly huge. Rent a serious breast pump and you will have relief in a matter of minutes (and a batch of milk to freeze for later). Even the best models (Medela makes the Lamborghini of breast pumps, in my humble opinion) are not very expensive to rent, and they're incredibly effective. My first afternoon home from the hospital, I was transformed from a whining heap of misery to an efficient and happy milk machine, a mere half-hour after my sister Kathy rushed out and brought a rental Medela home to me.

Your hospital should be able to provide you with the names of places that rent these machines, and I can't say enough about the difference it can make. And if you're trying to pump when you go back to work, rent the same machine again. Those little hand pumps are for masochists or people with a boatload more patience than I possess. I say go for the efficiency. Go for the power.

Third, nurse for as long as you can. Who knows when anybody will be so unabashedly enthusiastic about your breasts again? (But when the little guy can trot up, unbutton your blouse, and help himself, it's probably time to quit. You want to save some therapy time for the other 9,000 scarring things you'll do in the future.)

And if you want to rent a Medela pump and need the location of the source nearest you, consult Medela's Breastfeeding National Network or visit *www.medela.com.*

laura's breastfeeding hold-out rule

My mother was a breastfeeding nut, too, and alive to bug me about it, so I decided early in the game that no way was I going to nurse my son Patrick. Isn't that immature? But so satisfying! Actually, I did try for about a week, but it was agony. My son wouldn't latch on, he bit me constantly, and even though there were no teeth involved, it hurt. I just wasn't comfortable with the whole thing. It felt too intimate and clammy. I realize the health benefits of nursing, but I have to tell you, Patrick's the healthiest three-year-old you've ever seen, so I guess it didn't do him any harm. I say honor your feelings and don't get guilt-tripped into nursing if you can't stand it. What's the point of that?

RULE #55:
Nursing is not a contraceptive.
Let me repeat this. Nursing is not a form of birth control. In fact, I believe it's quite the opposite. I have no scientific evidence to back this up (please see the disclaimer at the beginning of the book), but I'm completely convinced that a woman's fertility soars right off the charts directly after birth—and I have at least four or five nieces and nephews to prove it. Don't think that just because you're nursing you are immune to this phenomenon. Even if it took you years to get pregnant—in

fact, *especially* if it took you years to get pregnant—when you least want to be pregnant again is when you're most likely to conceive. Who said Mother Nature doesn't have a sense of humor?

RULE #56:
Chin up.

This may either go down in the category of "Too much information, Betty" or "Thank goodness someone warned me." Whatever. For some bizarre reason, right after I gave birth, I developed a large patch of almost invisible, soft, white-blonde hair under my chin. I discovered it while glancing in the rearview mirror of my car when the sunlight was just grazing my profile, and I almost ran off the road. The soft hairs pulled right out—naturally, I was on the shoulder of the road, yanking them out by the roots while traffic swirled around me—but I noticed later that a couple of other women who had just given birth had the same thing. Check your chin and get out your tweezers. I felt like one of the Three Billy Goats Gruff—and who needs that?

RULE #57:
Wallow.

Fitness buffs may disagree (oh, go lift something), but this is no time to whip yourself back into shape. Or even whip yourself out of bed. Laze a little. Heck, laze a lot. For working moms, this precious time off is going to evaporate before you know it, so don't fill it up with things you've got to get done. Or a body you've got to rehabilitate. Same thing goes for moms working at home. There will be plenty of time to jog, tread, lift, run, pedal, push, and knead yourself back into a semblance of your pre-baby silhouette. Now is a good time to be as relaxed as possible so your baby's first days are gentle and slow and sweet. Like a river of molasses.

RULE #58:
Buy some cool bracelets.
Okay, I realize this may sound completely superficial. But you're going to end up with about 7,000 photos of your forearms—holding the baby, bathing the baby, nursing the baby, etc.—and if you are wearing beautiful bracelets, you're going to look like a glamorous mom. You may not feel terribly glamorous right now, but sometimes what you seem to be is what you will become. Which is sort of deep, now that I think about it.

RULE #59:
Get outta here. (Part II)
After Mr. Wrong made his exit, I was left with three months off work and a new baby to entertain. It didn't make much sense to hang around Denver, waiting to see whom he was going to date next, so I got Lulu a passport and took off to see

Sarah, my friend in England. I also cruised over to Barcelona, went East to visit my family, attended a high-school reunion, spent a couple of weeks in Montana, and took Lulu on a business trip to New York. Turns out I am exceptionally good at running away from my problems. And so is my daughter. Those gate departure announcements in airports became as familiar as nursery songs; Lulu was a born traveler.

I'm a huge advocate of traveling with newborns. For one thing, they can't complain about the museums you're dragging them to, or ask if you're there yet. They're completely mobile and get in everywhere free—just strap 'em to your chest and go. And if you're nursing, you've got everything the baby needs, right at your nipple tips. It's a wonderful time to travel!

Now granted, in England I was staying in a beautiful house in the countryside of Gloucestershire, had a friend who took great care of me without my quite realizing she was doing it, and had enough money to feel secure about doing all this. I realize that not everybody has that luxury. But if you (and your mate) can swing even a little time away, it's a lot easier now than it will be for the next, say, twenty years. Don't be afraid to take the Precious Bundle away from home, feeling like he will be disoriented or alienated. As long as you're relaxed, the baby will be just dandy. (Of course, if travel makes *you* feel disoriented or alienated, stay right in your own zip code. The idea is to get yourself to a place where you'll feel lovely—which for me was 5,000 miles from my laundry basket, household chores, and my real life.)

RULE #60:
Heads up.

Yes, you will lose a boatload of hair after giving birth. That's a given. But let's think positive about this: It gives you a perfect excuse to dye your hair if you've been afraid to use the chemicals, or to get a groovy new haircut. Get a babysitter or friend to watch the Precious Bundle and go get yourself a really expensive, lovely new hairdo that doesn't require a lot of maintenance. (Unless you're Katie Couric and you've got somebody doing your hair every morning, let's not get too optimistic here.) And while you're at it, buy every gorgeously packaged and fragranced hair thickener, strengthener, humectant, gel, and mousse you want. All things considered, it's a cheap thrill. And you're worth it.

RULE #61:
Develop a high gross-out threshold.

All baby books attempt to explain the unexpected things that babies do. What they don't tell you is how deeply freaky some of those maneuvers can be. The Moro startle reflex, for instance—terrifying when you first witness it! You undress the Precious Bundle, cooing and ooohing, and all of a sudden the baby throws its arms out wide and jerks as if you'd stuck her with an electric cattle prod. This is not entirely confidence-inspiring for a new, or even an experienced, mother.

Projectile vomiting is another case in point. Sure, I'd read about it. I understood the concept. But the day I bent over with

Lulu in my arms and she spewed out a rocket of baleen that blasted a full nine feet away, I was convinced she'd thrown up her large intestine. There was simply NO way a baby should do that.

Fevers, croup, ear infections . . . it's just unbelievable what this darling child is going to put you through. Fasten your seat belt. And pray you've got a strong stomach.

RULE #62:
Kiss your savings goodbye.

On my very first trip to the grocery store after having Lulu, I spent more than $100. My sister Kathy was with me. I almost passed out. I'd never spent $100 at the grocery store in my life, except on Thanksgiving. And to be honest, I don't think I've spent less than $50 on any trip since. Kids are expensive. Hideously, ridiculously expensive. Get used to it.

RULE #63:
L'chaim.

At some point when you've achieved consciousness again, take it upon yourself to open an expensive bottle of champagne with your partner or best friend and congratulate yourself on making it all the way through pregnancy, labor, delivery, and producing an amazing baby. (But if you're breastfeeding, confine yourself to one luscious glass.)

Job well done! Bottoms up!

Lovely Bubblies under $25 That Won't Break the College Fund

Compliments of Steven Kolpan, The Charmer Sunbelt Professor of Wines at The Culinary Institute of America

Prosecco, Mionetto, Veneto, Italy NV

Rose, Cristalino, Cava, Spain NV

Blanc de Noirs, Gruet, New Mexico NV

Blanc de Blancs, Domaine Ste. Michelle, Columbia Valley, Washington NV Brut

Roederer Estate, Anderson Valley, California NV Brut

Argyle, Willamette Valley, Oregon NV Brut

Seaview, South Eastern Australia NV Brut

Glenora, Finger Lakes, New York NV Blanc de Noirs

Domaine Chandon, Napa Valley, California NV Brut

Paul Chenau, Cava, Spain NV

(NV = non-vintage)

Bonus Pointer for Self-denial Moms: Be a care-taker.

Normally, I'm not someone who feels very comfortable being looked after. I'm a doer, not a do-ee, so I can understand any reluctance to follow this bit of advice. But just this one special time, make an exception. Practice saying, "I'd love that!" "That would be great!" and "Thanks so much!" It's not so hard once you get the hang of it.

An example: Mimi, her husband, and I went camping in the Colorado wilderness when Lulu was about two months old. I was nursing Lulu and reading my book by the fire when Mimi asked if I wanted a lavender-infused washcloth for my face because she was making one for herself. (Mimi is the Queen of Indulgence, which makes her the perfect friend to hang with. You're always assured great wine, lovely food, and girly luxuries like this, even at 10,000 feet above sea level.)

I looked up and said automatically, "No thanks . . . that's okay."

Suddenly I had an epiphany. Was I really saying, "No, I don't want the nice, warm, thick, lavender-infused washcloth that you've had the creativity and thoughtfulness to offer me, way up here in the pristine wilderness?"

Hello?

I started over again. "Mimi, I would love a lavender-infused washcloth. As soon as possible. Before you make one for yourself, in fact."

Let somebody take care of you. It will make them feel good. It will make you feel good. It will make your baby feel good—well, that's probably not true. But it's never too soon to start setting a good example of non-self-denial.

CHAPTER SIX

Mother Rules:
4 to 6 Months—
The Chrysalis Cracks

baby steps back to life

e nough slobbering sentimentality. Life is just about to hand you a healthy dose of reality to wake you from your charming, postbirth bliss. You may have to go back to work. You will probably have to figure out some sort of day care or play group activity. The Precious Bundle will start teething, rolling over, kicking—and generally getting ready for the job of his or her youth, which is to suck all the life out of you and then abandon you for college, sex, friends, and a fabulous future. You will be the empty, brittle, spent husk left on the ground beneath the wings of your lovely butterfly.

Okay, that may be a tiny exaggeration. And I might be just a tad premature with all the histrionics. By the time your adorable child does fly away, you'll probably be so ready to see him or her go, you'll happily agree to pay for tuition, room and board, and a better vehicle than the one you're driving. Anything to get that sullen, brooding hulk out of your house. Yes, it seems impossible to imagine now, looking into that cherubic little face. But if the Precious Bundle remained so darling and sweetly dependent, you'd never be able to let him go. He has to become more independent, self-sufficient, and eventually, unthinkably, even irritating—so you'll be able to release him to the world. This is called Growing Up, Phase 1. These Eleven Action-Packed Rules will help you stay sunny side up through it all.

RULE #64:
Welcome to Cutie-pieville.

Could your baby be any cuter? Gone is the baby acne—which, like a true mother, I swore Lulu never had (photos tell a different story). Gone are the crossed eyes, the spaced-out stares, the slobbering lumpishness, and lo and behold, the infant you thought could not be any more perfect has become a sturdy, chubby, glorious baby. You've got personality. You've got interaction. You've got coos and smiles and laughs. All in a package that is still, essentially, immobile. It doesn't get much better than this—with the exception of a few minor glitches.

RULE #65:
Hit the bottle.

Early on, I read a lot of stern admonitions about the importance of getting your baby accustomed to taking a bottle.

These articles grimly threatened that if you were too much of a lackadaisical backslider to get your baby accustomed to using a bottle during the first few months, she might very well *never take a bottle at all*. I loved breastfeeding so much, I just didn't have the heart to replace my own big, bountiful breasts with a cold, mechanical bottle. So by month 4, Lulu had never taken a bottle, I was going back to work, and Lulu was starting day care with Grammy Mary and was going to have to take my breastmilk from a bottle. Or *starve*. The stakes were sort of high. In a panic, I brought Lulu into work, where four of my male partners with children had volunteered to help her break through the bottle barrier. (You're supposed to have a male give the baby a bottle so no breasts will confuse her or raise her expectations.) One by one, my partners strode into the conference room, Lulu in their arms, confident of complete success. One by one, they came out dripping with sweat, irrefutably beaten. Lulu wore them all down in what I now recognize as a portent of the astonishing stubbornness with which she is blessed. All tried. All failed. Lulu was due at Grammy's the next day.

That morning, I walked up to the house, handed Lulu to Grammy Mary with my frozen bottles of breastmilk and confessed. "I have something really bad to tell you. Lulu has never, ever taken a bottle. And I'm afraid she never will."

I burst into tears. Mary burst out laughing, bundled Lulu and the bottles to her chest, and said, "When she's hungry she will." Then she firmly shut the door in my face. I called two hours later, convinced that Mary would ask me to pick up my starving child immediately. Lulu had had two bottles and was also eating some cereal. Her first solid food! I was missing half her life already.

RULE #66:
Take a powder.

This is not the time to go for the natural look. This is the time to use every trick in your cosmetic bag to make yourself feel good. Do it every day, as soon as you're getting up for real, and don't lose your momentum. Listen, if I can complete my five-minute makeup regime going 65 mph down the worst highway on the East Coast, you can get in there and slap on a little foundation, lipstick, and mascara at the very beginning of the day. (If you put it off, it will not occur to you, at 11 A.M. during your midmorning slump, to do so. By that time, you'll have gotten used to looking haggard.) Makeup can make a drastic difference in the way you feel about yourself when that darling stockboy falls into the apples trying to help you. Or when you have to say hi to that annoyingly slim mom who lives behind you and always looks perfect, even when she's just taking out the trash. Honestly. Hit the hard stuff.

RULE #67:
Affirm this.

Okay, this is a little bit of a self-help gimmick, but I'm not above that. Stick a note on your bathroom mirror reading,

"I am a great and fabulous mom!" Now, put on your makeup while you repeat that out loud. And each time you see your beautiful, bleary-eyed face, tell yourself what a lucky baby that child of yours is, to get you as a mother.

liz's "be a fortunate one" rule

Some people go to fortunetellers when they get confused or overwhelmed, and naturally, that's just what I did during this time of my baby's life. Which was so brain-dead, because the minute a psychic tells you something is going to happen, you can't help but believe, on some level, that it actually will. (Of course, if psychics know so much, why do they always live in those rundown little houses and have seriously tacky furniture?) I've got a better suggestion. Write your own fortune. Seriously. Write down ten blessings for which you are grateful. Then flip over the paper and write ten things that you desire in your life. Stick it in your purse and take it with you everywhere you go. In a year or two, pull it out. You may be surprised at how much closer you've come to achieving your stated intentions. You already *are* fortunate. That's the real secret.

RULE #68:

Get your monthly periodical.

Take out a magazine subscription as a little monthly present to yourself (consider it compensation for that other monthly present you get just for being a girl). Do not make it something challenging like *Atlantic Monthly* or *The New Yorker*, which actually require quite a bit of concentration, not to mention the ability to read consecutive paragraphs. That's a long way off for you, sister. Settle for *People* (which is weekly, but so inconsequential, who cares if you only read two pages?), *Vogue,* or *In Style*—something eminently browsable that will give you the sensation that you still have a shred of interest in fashion, culture, and the glam life. At all costs, I would avoid magazines that purport to tell you how to lead a more simple life by grinding your own grain or making damask headboards and matching valances. (The holiday issue of *Real Simple,* for instance, weighed in at a daunting 360 pages. How simple can it be?) The idea is to "read" a magazine that requires nothing more strenuous or intellectually demanding than flipping pages, and engenders emotions no more troubling than mild celebrity envy. You can handle that.

RULE #69:
Doing the day care thing.

If you work (Do I have to add *"outside the home?"* You know and I know that I have nothing but the utmost respect and yes, awe, for women who can stay at home with their children and not commit hari-kari or multiple acts of stenciling—and yes, I'm fully cognizant that we all work our fannies off; now can I get back to my point before I lose it?), then you will be faced, from here to eternity, with the *Sturm und Drang* of day care. When I first had Lulu, I used to think that my day care worries would last about two years. Then I thought, well, by the time she goes to school, I'll be set. Somehow—blissful ignorance?—I never considered that for the rest of her life at home, I was going to have to figure out a safe, secure, stimulating, dependable, structured, lovingly supervised place for her to be while I was busy earning a living. When she was seven months. When she was seven years. When she was seventeen—yikes! especially when she was seventeen. I was even going to have to cover summers. I remember the day it hit me like a sledgehammer of shame that she would probably never get to have one of those lazy, boring, interminable summers of hanging around the house, reading, sweating, playing Monopoly and biking to the pool, because I would be working. And she would be working, too, going to day care. For her entire childhood.

I don't think there is any guilt that quite compares to this. (Although the guilt of a broken home comes close, and unfortunately, I was able to provide that experience for Lulu, too.) It breaks your heart that at such a tender age, your child will be away from you for about nine hours, every workday. That's a long day. It's long for an adult. For a baby, it must seem like years. And then there's the stress of having to spend all that time with other people (even other babies), which, as we all know, is real work. I don't know what to say—it just sucks.

I had no choice about working; I had no child support for the first two years of Lulu's life, and I had a business to run. But I still feel as if Lulu paid the price for my going back to work. And maybe that's why I and a million other baby boomers indulge our kids so pitifully. Because we're so sorry we didn't give them what they really wanted—our time, attention, and the full measure of our lives. Oh, wah wah wah. Let's get off the pity train, shall we?

My advice, for the first years at least, is to try to find the smallest, most personal day care you can afford. I always half-wished that I had had someone come to the house, so at least Lulu wouldn't have had to be bundled off every morning and could have stayed at home. (Although that might have also meant I would have been able to work longer hours, and I really didn't want to enable myself to do that.) Instead, Grammy Mary watched Lulu and a baby boy in her sun-splashed and art-filled house for three years. Which was pretty great, all things considered. Consistency was hugely important to me. I had friends who hired nannies from Mexico—they were darling girls, every one, but because of immigration difficulties and family complications, it was a revolving door every six months. Because my life was so chaotic, I really wanted Lulu to have one thing that didn't change in her life. Something she could count on, which—unlike her parents—would stay predictably the same, day after day, year after year. Grammy was all that, and a bag of chips.

Obviously, this costs a boatload of money. Any day care does. When you're looking, think long and hard about what you want, then talk to anybody who will listen and ask if they can provide you with a lead to the kind of day care you've settled on. I ended up with Grammy Mary, who is also my friend Mimi's mom, because I was talking to Mimi and she mentioned that her mom was losing one of the babies she cared for, and had room for Lulu. That's the way it usually works. Serendipity. But serendipity doesn't work unless you're out there nosing around.

Let me reiterate one thing. I would strongly urge you to spend whatever you can afford to get the day care that gives you the greatest peace of mind. It may cost a lot now, but it's going to make you feel a whole lot better when you look back and know that the Precious Bundle was in good hands, even if the hands weren't always yours.

mary lou's home alone rules

The hardest thing when you're staying at home with your kids is trying to find the time to do all the things most people do at work. Like paying bills, reading the mail, talking on the phone, or arranging your schedule (meaning, your kids' schedule, around which your schedule will invariably be built). Personal time is almost impossible to carve out at home because of the fluidity of domestic work; it simply refuses to keep a shape or a timetable. Not to mention the kids themselves, who somehow just will not go away. The one thing I try to do is not answer the phone any time in the morning. And I force myself to stop doing chores and do something indulgent when the kids are napping. Sometimes I read a book, sometimes I take a bath, and sometimes I just put on my yoga tape and lie on the floor breathing—or more precisely, panting. It doesn't sound like a lot, but it makes a huge difference for me to take that time and claim it as my own. Look, just because there will always be laundry to do doesn't mean you always have to be doing laundry. If you don't figure this out, you'll never be able to stay home with your kids. You'll just lose your mind.

RULE #70:

Draw the line.

To make a staggering understatement, the world of business is not mommy-friendly. It's our job as mommies to make it more so. The only way to do this is to be as strident as possible about what you will and won't do. (In a really feminine and respectful manner, of course. Yeah, right.)

Take, for instance, the 7 A.M. meeting. These used to be called power breakfasts, until the obvious level of self-congratulation in the term became too embarrassing for even the most ego-infested corporate diners to use. The sole purpose of holding a 7 A.M. meeting, in my humble opinion, is to prove that you can get people to show up at this ungodly, family-unfriendly hour.

Just say no. As a single mother, I had to. For me to attend a 7 A.M. meeting meant I had to leave before Lulu was awake and pay a babysitter to sleep over, wake up with Lulu, then drive her to day care—all so I could sit there eating muffins with some MBA-hole? I don't think so. There was simply no way I was going to extend the amount of time my baby had to be in day care so that some guy (or gal; let's be honest, the power bug bites regardless of gender) could feel like he really got a jump on the day.

At first I was terrified to say I wasn't able to make a meeting, but I got over that pretty quickly. And soon, I got nothing but back-slapping support from my coworkers and co-mom clients who were previously too cowed by the meeting maniacs to say, "Hell, no, we won't go."

The key is productivity. If you're going to resist working early, late, and weekends, then you darn well better spend all your time at work actually working. This is far more difficult than it sounds. Built into every working day, I'm convinced, are two to three hours of pure Fooling Around Time. Cut the FAT, and you can get an amazing amount of stuff accomplished while you keep the time you spend at work to a reasonable eight or nine hours a day.

This means no soft landings when you arrive at the office—greeting everybody at the coffee machine and catching up on the plots of last night's television shows. You can also avoid wasting vast amounts of time if you cut back on personal phone calls at work and use your cell phone on the car ride home to catch up with friends. Need I remind anyone that e-mail is the devil's playground? And how about the time-chewing ravages of the long lunch? Bring food from home, grab a quick lunch at your desk, and you'll have almost an extra hour or two to get things done (like e-mailing your friends for a romance update).

Not that I've actually ever practiced any of these time management skills, except skipping lunches out, and that's just because I'm too cheap to spend the money on restaurants and I have a fatal attraction to the bread basket. In actual fact, I'm a notorious and shameless proponent of using work time to take care of your personal business (when else are you supposed to do it—during cocktail hour?), but I thought I'd pass along what I'd do if I were a really responsible type. My saving grace is that I work really fast. And I've found that as long as you're getting all your work done and being highly responsible (in other words, looking like you're working really hard), your credibility should remain high enough to allow you the flexibility to say no when you need to. (And now you really do have to buy this book for all your friends, because I absolutely will be fired.)

Lest you feel guilty that you're a woman and you're asking for special treatment, I've got one word for you: Golf. This is a sport that is practically a sacrament to most (male) corporate executives. As far as I can tell, its chief recommendation is that it makes one unavailable to one's spouse, kids, and employees for a good six hours. That's just for the eighteen holes—it doesn't take into account the après-golf rounds of gin, the watching of golf on TV, or the search for the perfect putter or wood.

Speaking of wood, I've got one more word: Sex. Scientific studies (who's getting these grants, anyhow, and how can I get one?) have shown that men's minds are mired in sexual fantasies about once every three minutes. Now that's a lot of downtime that's not being spent on out-of-the-box thinking. So don't sweat your supplication for an eight- or nine-hour day. It's nothing!

michelle's latte rule

When my kids were babies, I used to hire a babysitter for two or three hours so I could go out and have a coffee. I didn't use that time productively to balance my checkbook or to pay bills; I just sat there in Starbucks and sipped my latte and felt like the freest bird on the planet. I loved that I could do that. On the way home, I'd pick up a box of luscious chocolates and a new CD to prolong the feeling that I was a real person with musical tastes and a refined palate—a feeling that would flee the instant I walked back in the door of my house and my little monsters leeched themselves back onto my legs. But it was great while it lasted.

RULE #71:
Expect a few aftershocks.

When I went back to work, I had to put on clothes. Real clothes. Previously I had managed, by the grace of overalls and elastic-band skirts, to delude myself that my pregnancy weight had simply fallen away. As if. The first time I tried to close a proper waistband, I was horrified to find the two ends a good three inches apart. Good God! Who the hell had shrunk my favorite pants? A couple of outfits later, I was forced to come to the obvious conclusion that I was still quite a bit more rotund than before this party started. Perhaps I'd placed a tad more emphasis than necessary on getting my full quota of nursing calories?

Another reality bite: You're going to have to start working out again. Diligently. With a focus on your pillow parts: abs, butt, arms, etc. It's a drag, but it's either that, or buy all new clothes. Sit-ups are cheaper. And believe it or not, you'll feel better when you do work out. All those endorphins and whatnot coursing through your veins.

If you can't make it to the gym, you can always make it to your bedroom floor; there's a plethora of home DVDs that

Home Exercise Workouts that Work

Having resorted to working out at home for years, off and on (okay, mostly off), I consider myself an expert in what makes a good home workout video. A few things to look for:

The great outdoors.
Because it's sort of pathetic (let's face it) to be lying on your living room floor working out, the very least you can expect is an exotic location or pretty scenery to peruse.

Celebrity bods.
Sure, it's trite beyond belief, but they are celebrities because they're great to look at and presumably laden with charisma, both of which should help you and/or shame you into doing your crunches.

Multiple workouts.
Sometimes you have forty-five minutes to devote to a workout and sometimes you have fifteen. Look for more than one time option on a tape.

Not too much instruction.
When you've watched the tape eighty-eight times, a lot of "Here's how you lift the weight, ladies!" is going to get seriously annoying.

Avoid dance routines.
This tip is a direct result of my own scarring Paula Abdul Dance Workout fiasco.

Not too easy.
Or you'll be bored to tears in a week.

Not too difficult.
If it completely overwhelms you, you'll immediately "lose" the tape in the back of the entertainment center.

Well-organized content.
It should be easy to pop in the tape or DVD, find the workout you want, and go. Otherwise, you'll lose valuable workout time (oh darn).

Good music.
This is huge. Luckily, celebrities are usually sleeping with musicians, so their tapes have decent music.

Maximum effect for minimum effort.
Why the eight-minute workouts that feature none of the above amenities are still incredibly useful.

will help whip you back into shape. The important thing is to find a tape you like and just do it. However, a much more indulgent route (and hence, one you're more likely to stick with) is to join a gym that offers child care. Even when you couldn't care less about climbing on the StairMaster, the idea of getting someone else to watch the Precious Bundle for an hour or two is likely to be irresistible. Men, also, are exceedingly partial to gyms, possibly due to the high incidence of lycra involved, so you can expect a lot of spousal support for this expenditure.

RULE #72:
Know the limits of man.

As you come out of the cocoon of your baby's infancy and the demands on your time become ever more urgent, you may notice something rather odd about your husband (although very perceptive women may pick up on its latent manifestation years earlier). Lulu's dad wasn't around much during daylight hours for me to observe, so it wasn't until I remarried and inherited three stepchildren and a six-bedroom home that I truly experienced the male habit I call "*chores interruptus.*" After seven itchy years, it continues to mystify and mesmerize me on a daily basis. Here's how to recognize its onset:

My husband, a helpful and thoughtful man (but thoroughly manly, to be sure) always unpacks his suitcases immediately upon coming home from a trip. He then takes the suitcases and places them carefully on the stairs to the third floor, where they will sit for days, weeks even, until finally I break down and carry them up to the third floor closet where they are stored. This routine never, ever fails. He has never, to my knowledge, actually completed the task of putting the luggage away. The laundry? Slap-dash folded and left on the top of the dryer. Pots and pans? Washed and left dripping on the stovetop. The toilet paper? Never, ever replaced on the roll—in fact, rather than go all the way to the other bathroom and get a fresh roll, he will work his way through multiple and expensive boxes of Kleenex.

But I don't take it personally.

Each evening, my sister's husband methodically clears every dinner plate from the table, rinses them, and places them in the dishwasher. Yet in twenty-three years of marriage, he has never cleared a single piece of silver or glass. Does he not see them, gleaming on the table? Is this some kind of cutlery phobia?? Who knows?

My friend Abbie's husband will never fail to carefully fold a sopping wet bath towel into the size of a handkerchief and then force the fat wad over the towel rack, thereby ensuring almost instantaneous mildew. Astonishing!

Now, it doesn't take a brain surgeon to figure out that laundry, saucepans, and suitcases don't fly back to where they belong all by themselves. (In fact, I'd be willing to bet that male brain surgeons manifest some of the worst symptoms of *chores interruptus*.) So what is it with men? Are they simply not aware that a task needs completion? Is it a mere lack of consciousness that you, the wife, will then be forced to complete the chore for them, time after time? Or is it something deeper and more sinister?

It's that last one. Any wife worth her salt has no doubt pleaded, begged, cajoled, nagged, and eventually screamed at her husband to stop quitting the task before it's done—and to no avail. So how are we to understand why, just when we need them the most, our husbands will develop this habit of *chores interruptus?* (Which, by the way, much like the other *interruptus*, can have a really negative impact on your sex life.) My theory is that men in a challenging domestic situation do a bit of work, and then, like a circuit breaker that's been overloaded, reach their limit and just shut down. Some insidious boundary inside is telling them, "You've done enough, just stop, have a beer, take a shower, watch a little TV." And they listen to that little voice inside and obey. Unfortunately, the little voice inside most women is telling them, "Get it done. Don't rest until you're through. If you don't do it now, it'll still need doing tomorrow. Get it done. Get it done. Get it done."

So who do you think ends up getting it done? The one unwinding in front of the TV, or the one on overdrive who's not going to stop until the last sock is matched up, the last suitcase carted upstairs, and the last dish wiped? That's right, momma. There's no limit to the work we do. Until finally, we drop into bed just as our mate turns to us with a twinkle in his eye, hoping for some uninterrupted marital affection. At which point, chances are enormously high that a little voice inside is going to say, "You've done enough for one day, don't even think about it, turn over, get some sleep."

Firestarters for Burned Out Mommies

1. Baby sitter
2. Wine
3. Clean hair, fresh bikini wax, spanking clean bod
4. Lingerie *you* like
5. Conversation
6. Racy movies (and I'm not talking NASCAR here)
7. Music
8. Soft (forgiving) lighting
9. Time
10. A spirit of adventure and a sense of humor

RULE #73:

Getting it on . . . and other dim memories.

Speaking of the frequency of your marital relations, this can be a bit of a difficult time. Many women experience an ebbing of desire as their passion for sleep eclipses the lust for sex by about a billion percent. Many men find this attitude dispiriting and strive to find solace in the arms of a La-Z-Boy or, far worse, a Slee-Z-Girl. Clearly, this is an area that requires some attention. I'm not sure I'm qualified to render an opinion (in fact, I know I'm not, but why should that stop me?) but I do think that each side has a valid point. Dad needs to do more, so Mom can sleep. And Mom needs to do Dad more, so he doesn't lose the will to live.

One helpful suggestion: Get away, if only for an evening. It sounds trite, but you really do need to put the baby out of your mind before you can get busy with each other. This is easier said than done, thanks to the constant presence of the infernal baby monitor, which puts the baby front and center in your brain and earshot at all times. In the home, where you are first and foremost a mother—with all the psychic baggage that entails—it can feel uncomfortable, if not downright illegal, to be the lewd and lascivious bedmate your husband so fondly remembers. Find somebody you trust implicitly to stay with the baby and go out, or better still, take an overnight trip away. There's nothing like leaving the Precious Bundle at home to light your fire. Got a match?

RULE #74:
The importance of fancy pants.

Before Cinderella could go out and hook up with Prince Charming (or even find someone to talk to other than the vegetables and mice), she had to get out of her nasty old cleaning clothes and into a ball gown. Does this tale resonate with you? Well, Cinderella had her fairy godmother, and you've got . . . *me.* And I'm here to tell you that the single greatest boost you can give your nightlife (other than turning off the TV and getting that lummox of a mate off the sofa) is to have three or four glam outfits at the ready in the back of your closet. This is not remotely difficult to accomplish. It just takes commitment. You have to be on the lookout for dazzling eveningwear everywhere you go—not actively or obsessively—but with a lizard's vigilant awareness of flies. (In the event you are not an inveterate shopper, relax. This is not a chronic task you need to perform; it's simply an emergency preparation kit you must create and periodically refresh.) When you are frantically looking for a dress-up outfit, you will *never* be able to find one and this will inevitably solidify your resolve never to shed your sweatpants again. Shop for eveningwear when you don't need it, and you'll find the kind of lovely stuff that will enable you to be ready for a party at the drop of a boa—and how fabulous is that?

Hit the vintage clothing shops and check out old evening gowns, sequined tops, and velvet jackets. Engage the women— or better still, gay guys—working there in your treasure hunt, and you'll fire up the kind of *esprit de corps* that makes shopping an invigorating romp. It's a bore working in retail, but when someone comes in ready for dress-up, what could be more fun?

Whenever you're traveling, nip into wild little boutiques you'd never venture into on a normal day. Troll for groovy old rhinestone jewelry at flea markets or street fairs. Even when you're out on a mundane mission to score a new oven mitt at the mall, take a brief spin around the eveningwear department. Dress-up clothes are constantly on sale (because no one's taking my advice!) and there's no reason why you shouldn't be the one to score the $400 dress marked down to $40. If you can acquire a couple pairs of gorgeous and sexy black pants, a fabulous skirt, and a dress that makes you feel drop-dead beautiful, plus a few tops that make you look stupendous but do not require you to be at your absolute thinnest, you'll be set. As for nursing moms, I would suggest flaunting the décolletage as much as possible with a plunging-neckline blouse atop a simple skirt or pants. At all costs, I would avoid the flowered mumu and other Earth Mother nursing outfits.

My goal is to be able to walk into my closet, filthy-dirty from the garden, and be able to walk out again looking passably glamorous in twenty minutes or less. Follow my simple shopping regimen and you'll likewise be able to transform yourself on command. Bibbity-bobbity-boo!

Bonus Pointer for Frugal Moms:
Go a little crazy.

While I was in England with baby Lulu, my friend Sarah, an unashamed and unabashed shopping enabler, took me to all the sweet little shops in Cheltenham, Gloucestershire County. This is one of the places where the royal family goes when they're bored with Westminster and Scotland. In no way could it be mistaken for an outlet mall. Everything is incredibly lovely. And ridiculously expensive. I found myself in a darling little dressing closet, trying on a hand-beaded white velvet and vintage-lace jacket that cost three times as much as Lulu's and my roundtrip airfare. It was a real "one-off," as Sarah said. Knowing how bad I was feeling about myself, she really, really wanted me to have it. She was relentless. I did buy it. I've worn it exactly three times. It is gorgeous and completely unnecessary. I'm not even sure if I'll ever wear it again, because it actually doesn't fit me very well. But it was a significant purchase, and one I've never once regretted.

This is an unlikely, and hence very healthy time for you to splurge on something wildly impractical. It can remind you of what else is out there. It can remind you that you're still fabulous.

CHAPTER SEVEN

Mother Rules:
7 to 10 Months—
The Great Leap Forward

quick, while they're still not walking . . .

t his is the dimple stage. The time when your baby is right on the verge of so many changes, he is a little fireball of excitement and anticipation. And so are you. Because while the Precious Bundle is fully alert, responsive, noisy, and way beyond adorable, he will still stay pretty much wherever you put him— which is so considerate! This blissful confluence of likeability and immobility is fleeting, so take full advantage of it. If you're one of those parents of an early-achieving baby (the kind who walks at eight months), pat yourself on the back and tell yourself how lucky you are to have a prodigy. (Maybe it was all those Einstein tapes?) Of course, all that early walking *really* means is you got cheated out of a good two to three months of rest and relaxation and will have to run around 50 percent more than other parents. But hey, genius has its price tag. And you're paying it.

123

To help guide you through the thickets of decisions coming your way about sleep, food, manners, and mental health, here are a Dozen Dazzling Rules to Live By.

RULE #75:
Smile.

I firmly believe that the faces babies look into are the faces they will imitate. Or, to put it in a more cosmic way (I once read this on the back of a Celestial Seasonings tea box): "What you love you will come to resemble." So when you're staring into your baby's face, be expressive. Show your joy. Let your own light shine. And surround your baby with people and caregivers who are so full of life, it spills over in their eyes and grins. Granted, every baby comes with his or her own personality, but I'm amazed at how many solemn, serious babies are the offspring of moody, serious adults. Happiness is contagious. Give it away.

And if you're feeling too grim for words, go back and read Rule #33, and rent every movie on that list until you start feeling human again.

RULE #76:
Enough with the Family Bed.

Don't even get me started on this one. Let's go back for one minute to when you were a kid—back when parents didn't have the slightest twinge of guilt about damaging their kids' fragile self-esteem or wounding their spirits. (When my dad, for instance, thought any of the eight of us were getting a little too self-confident, he used to promise, "I'm going to take you down a peg or two!" And he did, too. In fact, it's a wonder I have any pegs left.)

Now, can you imagine your dad thinking it would be a splendid idea for you to sleep with him and your mom for, say, the next five years? Of course not. That would mean he wouldn't get any sleep, he wouldn't get to spread out, he wouldn't get any. No way were you putting so much as a little baby toe across the threshold of the marital boudoir. But today, we're so bloody insecure and we've read so many helpful books, we've lost any kind of common sense—not to mention the protective custody of our own personal space. Where did we get the idea that learning to sleep in one's own bed is a peculiar kind of torture? Under the guise of sensitivity, we're far more likely to be giving our kids a lifelong sleeping problem. Not to mention the fact that it's difficult to be fabulous (and retain your dewy, youthful skin) if you're utterly sleep deprived.

Be a little selfish and claim your bed for your own and the nighttime as your friend. Set a positive example for your child that one is entitled to one's own bed, one's own privacy, and one's own pillow (and the certainty that one is *not* the loneliest number).

I have heard brilliant, compassionate, lovely friends of mine complain that they can't "make" their three-year-old go to bed, and so they all routinely stay up until midnight. Needless to say, the mom is too exhausted to have another baby or go back to work, the dad is cranky and depressed because he hasn't gotten laid in about two years, and the kid is hypersensitive and . . . sleepy.

The hand that rocks the cradle rules the world. Who's rocking your cradle? Think about it.

A **Nightmarish** Alternative

If you can't bring yourself to establish reasonable sleeping habits now, you may be forced, like my husband and his charming ex, to follow this routine when the child is two:

1. Every night, stand with your hand on the baby's back until he falls asleep.
2. Quietly walk toward the door, until the baby realizes you're leaving and wakes up howling.
3. Lie on the floor, talking quietly to him, until at last he falls asleep.
4. Sleep on the baby's floor all night, lest he hear you leaving and wake up howling.
5. Every night, repeat this process, moving two inches closer to the door, until approximately two years later, your child has learned to sleep all by himself.

Disregard *this* routine, and you may find yourself like another friend of mine whose eight-year-old wakes up every single night at 2 A.M., wanders into his parents' bedroom, and then insists that one of them return to his bedroom with him to sleep for the rest of the night. What's he going to do when he gets married? Drive over and pick one of them up?

RULE #77:
Find a need and feed it.

Lest you think I'm a big fat meanie (I am), wait until you hear this. I also don't think you should give your baby too much choice in what he eats. It's confusing for a baby to have to decide if he wants bananas or tapioca. Heck, I still can't choose between them. When I was visiting my friend Rachel up in Montana, I watched her brother-in-law stand in front of an open refrigerator for a good fifteen minutes, running through the entire contents for his two-year-old, hoping to settle on a desirable breakfast entrée for the lad.

"Chad, would you like some orange juice? Apple juice? Tomato? How about some nice, cold grape juice, Chad? Or would you prefer chocolate milk? Maybe a yogurt? Or some fruit salad and a bagel? Oh, here are some eggs—I could make you some scrambled eggs. Or how about some blueberry waffles? Chad???" I almost made a citizen's arrest for mental cruelty to anybody within earshot. Chad, of course, loved it. Who wouldn't want their food choices to merit four hours of rapt attention a day?

Of course, I was raised in the Mother Teresa School of Culinary Denial, so maybe I'm just exhibiting a little sour grapes jealousy. With eight kids, our household operated on military efficiency. Choice was a laughable luxury we couldn't afford—along with name brands, packaged snacks, and more than one sliver of meat per person. On Monday, Wednesday, and Friday, my mom served eggs for breakfast. On Tuesday and Thursday, it was hot cereal. On Saturday, you could have unsweetened cereal, and on Sunday, the Lord's Day, you could live it up with a small bowl of sugared cereal and one piece of cinnamon toast. Every dinner featured a meat, a starch, a hunk of iceberg lettuce, and a frozen or canned vegetable, followed by a dessert of canned fruit or Jell-O. Astoundingly, we all survived and are, in fact, healthy as horses. We share a pathetic inclination to stockpile canned goods and are lifetime members of the Clean Plate Club, but other than that, our upbringing seems to have left no visible scars. Obviously, I have no experience of coddling around food and perhaps this accounts for my stingy reluctance to dish it out. Even so, I really don't believe it's in your child's best interest to give him the impression that the world is his deli.

RULE #78:
The world is your deli.

You, on the other hand, should give yourself as many delectable food choices as possible. Find the swishiest store in your neighborhood and develop the habit of stopping in there and dropping some serious dough. Or just go to your nearest Dollar Store and treat yourself to something indulgent. It's the least you can do to compensate yourself for becoming invisible. (Have you ever wondered what's up with that? Men used to follow me out in parking lots to try to chat me up, and it's not because I'm so darn cute. It's just *men*. But once I had a babe in arms, I could have strolled naked through the condom aisle and not one guy would have glanced in my direction. It's sort of liberating and sort of depressing at the same time. In any case, it still merits a compensatory cartload full of yummy, easy-to-prepare goodies on a weekly basis.)

Moms can develop the truly horrible habit of eating what's left on their children's plates—and with the exception of juice (which, as my friend Mary Kaye astutely noted, a splash of vodka almost makes palatable), it's a nasty business. Break yourself of that tendency with a grown-up plate full of gorgeous mixed olives, a stunning little hummock of Stilton cheese, or some breathtakingly fresh asparagus. Search out places where you can lavish yourself with treats, and still look your checkbook in the face afterward. Indulge.

lulu's reality bite

Get real. My mom never, ever throws any food away. It's disgusting. She's like a human garbage disposal, the way she'll eat my leftover eggs and Tyler's leftover salad. She and Larry fight over our toast crusts. My mom needs to take her own advice and stop eating our leftovers before she embarrasses me to death.

RULE #79:
Don't table the manners.

As soon as she got big enough to eat more than Pablum, I had Lulu eat pretty much what I did. That seemed to work well for both of us, since after nine hours at work I was not about to cook a meal of which she'd eat approximately three tablespoons. You might also be forewarned: Food is the first big control game kids learn to play. The more you seem to be invested in getting them to eat something, the more likely they are to reject it, if only to see how great a response that will generate. I wasn't that invested in getting Lulu to eat oysters or anything weird, because my tastes are fairly pedestrian (okay, totally pedestrian, but that's entirely due to the way I was raised—see Rule #77), and luckily she was a good eater from the start. My biggest mistake was impatience. If Lulu was the slightest bit willing to eat, I'd shovel food in her mouth at a blinding speed, afraid the opening would close, I guess. And to this day, she will still shovel stuff in—half a hot dog, huge mouthfuls of pasta, an entire banana. She eats like a truck driver (I hereby apologize to any and all offended truck drivers, whom I sincerely admire and feel indebted to for our great system of transportation, even when I'm busy cutting them off or pulling out in front of them on the highway), and it's all my fault. So just know: It's never too early to start with table manners, and it's always too late to rehab a picky eater.

ginger's totalitarian food regime

The way we eat in this country is pretty revolting. And we've got the chubby, sedentary kids to prove it. I hope I won't horrify anybody here, but I make my kids eat what I make and there's really no negotiation about it. If you don't want it, it's like, okay, well then you just get a smaller helping. I try to always serve lots of fresh vegetables, fruits, and good protein instead of packaged and processed foods, and I constantly kick my kids outdoors to make them get some exercise. Here's Clue #I about food: If you don't buy crap, they can't eat crap. I always have tons of great food in the house, and I'm constantly offering my kids healthy snacks and lots of water. Not buying the bad stuff is the easiest way to control your kids' diet. It's not rocket science.

RULE #80:
Let the competition begin.

Right about now, you're going to be getting to know a lot of other mommies—in playgroups, on the playground, and everywhere in between. This will inevitably lead to conversation about your babies, which will inevitably lead to chatter about who's doing what, which will inevitably lead to the Great Baby Competition. The queasy, anxious feelings that accompany this competition are impossible to avoid, unless your child is a true prodigy on every level. But God is fair and doesn't actually let that happen. So you can prepare yourself now for the terrible shock of realizing that your baby, previously thought to be utterly perfect, is in truth, *falling behind in some very serious ways!* This is natural.

I hate to break it to you, but your baby is not going to be the best, or the first, at everything. Sorry. Some babies out there are going to get their teeth first, crawl first, walk first, talk first, and yes, even read first. If you let it start bothering you now, sister, you're going to lose your mind come kindergarten. On the other hand, it's perfectly normal to worry.

Worry is a mother's most natural state of mind. The paranoia of a double agent is nothing compared to the unleashed apocalyptic imagination of a competitive mother. It goes something like this:

Chris's mom says that he already knows the entire alphabet, and Hannah's mom says she is singing nursery songs from start to finish, and Nathaniel's mom says he can identify sixteen different categories of dinosaurs, and my baby isn't even talking? Sure, he says a few words, but that doesn't come close to singing lyrics, for crying out loud. Okay, we're looking at tutors, private schools, remedial reading, and no more TV at all— not even Barney, and especially not those Teletubbies, they're probably sucking out his intelligence every time he watches them. I knew I shouldn't go back to work, this is all my fault, my kid is going to be flipping burgers at age thirty, and it's all my fault, but he really seems okay to me, but then of course he does, I'm just too blind to see that he's got real problems and he's crying out for help. Oh sure, he can hang upside down by his knees for fifty-five straight minutes, but what the hell kind of talent is that, he's going to put that on his college application next to his 450 SAT scores? We're totally screwed here, but he really seems so cute and so happy . . . what am I doing wrong and why are all the other kids so accomplished, and who do their parents think they are bragging about all the crap their kids can do, that is such bad manners and who cares anyway, my baby is much cuter than all theirs put together and he's sweet and darling, too, and he's his own person and this is not a competition. He's a great kid! But if he doesn't start talking in full sentences pretty soon, we're never coming to this stupid park again.

Excellent! Now you're in the swing of things. Only problem is, you're just going to work yourself up into a lather, and it won't accomplish a thing. Go back to Chapter 1 and reread the Bonus Pointer for High-Achieving Moms: There was only one Einstein. Or more fun still, take a field trip to Target and look at the people buying all those baby intelligence boosters. Do they really look like they're about to produce the next Stephen Hawking? Rent *Parenthood* and watch Steve Martin agonize over his kids' accomplishments. Rent *Baby Boom* and watch Diane Keaton feel inadequate about getting her one-year-old into a private school in Manhattan. The happy ending is that everybody eventually learns to relax and accept (sometimes forcibly) that their child is going to be good at some things, and not so good at others. And no, you don't get to choose for your child in the great talent pool of life. But then again, neither did your parents. Think about it.

RULE #81:

Get beyond the crawl.

A lot of parents get really exercised about the sequence of development—and possible psychological consequences of any variation from the norm. At seven months, Lulu had such a cute and bizarre way of flailing all her limbs about

while lying on her back, I was loath for it to end—even for
the greater good of walking. Her crawl was more of a scoot—
one leg dragged behind, one foot hopping forward, and both
arms motoring along like mad. I don't believe she ever prop-
erly crawled; one day she just stood up and staggered about.
Perhaps she's still waiting to show signs of this developmental breach, but I believe that, much like the hysteria over
bonding in the first minutes of the baby's life, the brouhaha
over crawling is unnecessary. However and whenever your
child gets to the upright *homo sapiens* state, it's all good. Take
it easy.

RULE #82:
Deal with disapproval.
Contrary to popular opinion, a woman's most powerful urge
is not to sleep with Brad Pitt (but that's close). It's to judge
other mothers' parenting skills. I do it. You do it. We all do
it—which is one reason why having children can be so harrowing. After all, the product of your love, parental effort, and
entire gene pool is right out there on display, quite possibly
picking his nose or scratching his private parts, for anybody
to judge or find lacking. This critical opprobrium is twice as
likely if you're having more fun, earning more money, or looking decidedly more fabulous than other mothers. Then you
and the Precious Bundle are bound to come under some serious scrutiny. You suspect that other mothers are watching you,
looking for the deleterious effects of your questionable maternal

skills on your child, and you're pretty darn sure you're falling seriously short on a daily basis.

Well, of course you are. We *all* are, even the Martha Stewarts who walk among us. Your only protection is to stop waiting for the disapproval to disappear, and start developing a thicker skin. It's time to toughen up, sweetheart. Tell yourself that you're doing the best you can and that's got to be enough.

For added ammunition, it helps to remember that a lot of things that are troublesome in a child (and hideously embarrassing to a parent) prove to be tremendous assets in adulthood. Do you really think Picasso was a well-behaved and normal kid? How about Madonna, or Ted Turner? Even Bill Gates dropped out of college. Love your child and don't look over your shoulder. You're doing *fine*.

RULE #83:
Play around.

It's time to get out there. Find the best park in your neighborhood, and get your baby familiar with going there. Make sure it's one that feels safe, has a nice selection of playground equipment, and is pleasingly green, because you'll be spending a lot of time there over the next three to five years. And don't forget the obvious benefit of a café nearby, where you can get a nice coffee and a magazine to keep you from dying of boredom. A park within walking distance is a definite bonus because, as you might have noticed, getting in and out of the car is becoming a huge production. (What moron designed an infant car seat that requires parents to clamber halfway into the back seat, hoist their butts in the air, and shove their heads into the seat to fasten the clip anyhow?) Even if it's farther afield, a good park is your escape from feeling housebound and always a destination of interest for your baby—so it's worth the search. You might not do much more than stick your Precious Bundle in the sandbox right now, but pace yourself. Big things are coming.

RULE #84:
Stop time.
Sure, you've got the camcorder. I'm here to remind you to *use it.* Take movies. Lots of them. Capture all the mundane little moments that couldn't possibly interest anyone except a mother (or grandparents). Don't edit your films until later, and never let anybody tell you that you're being overly sentimental or a cinematic pain in the butt. (Of course you are both, but who cares?) As vivid and unforgettable as this first year of life is, I promise you will never be able to remember precisely how it was—until you pop in the video ten years hence and are instantly transported back into your now-strapping child's infancy.

Case in point: Every year, Lulu and I watch her baby movies on her birthday. We spend hours wrapped in a time warp, happily reliving the past. Last year my husband came in, looked at the two kids talking and playing on the videotape for a couple of minutes and casually asked, "Who's that with Lulu?" "Um, that would be Tyler," I replied. "Your son."

You think you never will, but it's inevitable that you'll forget the lispy sound of your child's baby voice, the lovely shape of her baby body, and the heartbreaking beauty of his baby smile—until a movie brings it all back.

It's a mother's ultimate time machine. But it only works if you have the movies. Take the movies.

RULE #85:
Dress 'em up.

In about eighteen months, your child will refuse to wear anything you think looks adorable on her. This will continue for the rest of her life. Therefore, you have a very small window of opportunity here to dress the Precious Bundle in all the cute, sweet, darling, creative outfits you can find. Knock yourself out. Put those dumb curlicue ribbons in her hair. Buy ridiculous snowsuits with winged shoulders and bunny ears. Go for the sailor suit that makes him look like a mini Gene Kelly. Spend a small fortune on socks. Little hand-knit cotton sweaters? Absolutely. Ruffles on her diaper covers? Why not! You have your own personal little Barbie or Ken doll and right now, you can make him or her wear anything you want. Babies can't sue you or take you to court to sever your parental rights; they can't even talk! So have at it.

Just don't take too many photos of your handiwork or they'll be furious with you retroactively. Trust me on this.

RULE #86:
It doesn't really take a village.

An acquaintance of mine who had a baby rather late in life apparently read this wonderful African adage (Hillary Clinton borrowed it) and took it literally, then became utterly distraught when her village didn't behave the way she wanted it to. Her parents wouldn't move back from Florida, her husband wouldn't scurry out of corporate meetings to help her change a diaper, and her friends actually preferred to go out to lunch rather than gather at her house to admire her young lad. For those who are likely to have similarly inflated

The Repetitive Beauty of Repetition

I once read something in a dorky parenting newsletter that did more for my peace of mind and parental equilibrium than almost anything else I've encountered (except for that excellent bottle of Opus One). To paraphrase, it said kids use *behavior* to communicate, and the process of teaching them to shift from behavior to speech in expressing their feelings is essentially *developmental*. It went on to say that to learn how to communicate effectively, children will need *years* of guidance and positive modeling. Sure, some lessons they will learn right away, but others you will have to repeat, continuously, for *years*. That made me feel so good! Lulu wasn't thick as a brick. She was *learning*. Somehow that made it easier to say—not scream—"Please don't lick the pavement, honey" for the 533rd time. Maybe it'll work the same for you.

expectations: The saying is a *metaphor*. It doesn't really mean that you need an entire coterie of people to support your efforts in bringing up baby. Actually, you are quite capable of doing it on your own, and feeling confident about that is really half the battle. If you have grandparents, parents, extended family, and witch doctors in your village, fantastic. If all you have is yourself and a friend or two, that's perfectly adequate as well. It takes a mother. The village is gravy.

Sarah's caveat

However, if people really have their hearts set on doing everything for you—or you can possibly guilt-trip anyone into assuming that position—sit back, relax, and let them at it! Don't fight the feeling. (And please send me an e-mail explaining your methodology.)

Bonus Pointer for Working Moms:
Steering around the many roads to ruin.

Okay, it appears that in this chapter, I fell right in the trap that we're trying so hard to resist—focusing on your mommy side, without really talking about *you*, the woman who used to look amazing in a thong—or even if you didn't, had that potential if you ever decided to commit to a real workout and eat nothing but broccoli ever again. Anyhow, what about you? Have you completely disappeared into mommydom, and if so, how can we bring you back?

It's somewhat easier, of course, when you go back to work because then you have a few hours every day when you're not, first and foremost, a *mom* but instead become a *worker*. I'm not entirely sure this is a step in the right direction, but it does mean you can just waltz out the door in the morning and say, "Sorry, I really don't have time to pick you up and wipe your nose again, sweetheart, because I have to go to a meeting right this minute and no, I really don't have time to see that lovely mouthful of Cheerios that you've chewed up so well, darling, now please let go of my leg before my fabulous high heel scratches you, precious." At least it's amusing to contemplate doing that heartless Katharine Hepburn thing.

Work can help you regain your equilibrium and sense of self if for no other reason than when you don't have a baby attached to your hip, you're free to think about more insignificant, less emotionally jarring things than whether that weird orange stain on junior's tummy is sweet potato residue or the beginnings of smallpox. Work also can provide positive reinforcement, as when coworkers say, "Hey, good work on the Robertson job! I love what you did on that strategy briefing!" When you stay at home, nobody's admiring the way you fold the laundry, or saying, "Hey, good job on the groceries today! Way to work your magic at the deli counter!!" That's just not going to happen. Of course, we have repeatedly mentioned the repetitive nature of housework, which also tends to make one want to commit suicide (or homicide) on a daily basis.

The sad part of this tradeoff is that when you finally do call it a day and go back to work, you don't escape domestic hell.

You just get to experience it *in addition* to your eight-hour day . . . when you *get home from work*. I once read a chilling research statistic stating that working women spend almost as much time interacting with their children as do stay-at-home moms—only about twenty fewer minutes a day. They simply sleep a whole lot less, clean as little as possible, and do absolutely nothing for themselves. If you choose to go back to work, of course, you will also be swimming in guilt for every hour you haven't spent attending to your child's needs, and those laps can be fairly difficult to handle. I myself came to the conclusion that my current household of four children and husband would operate infinitely better if I didn't work. But after two very enjoyable and rewarding years spent at home, I was climbing the walls, literally, to stencil every surface in sight, and that seemed to be a tiny signal that I needed to go back to work. But now we're talking about *me* again, and we're supposed to be concentrating on *you*.

What can I tell you? I'm not sure there is a surefire solution, other than to fight like crazy to stay in love with your husband so he'll do lots of things to help you. Try to read as much as possible, so you don't feel that your brain has dried up like the prunes you now need to eat. And take regular breaks to get out and complain to your women friends. I mean this sincerely. I left every single one of my fabulous women friends in Colorado when I moved to Philadelphia to marry my husband, and the girlfriend deprivation alone almost killed me. Your women friends will bring you perspective, a forum, and a sense of humor that you cannot get in any magazine or book, not even this one. They'll remember the fabulous you that existed before the Precious Bundle stormed on the scene, and remind you of that stupendous woman when you drift too far into self-negating motherhood. Keep every one of your women friends as close as lint on a sweater.

CHAPTER EIGHT

Mother Rules:
10 to 12 Months—
Big Changes Ahead

breaking loose

Well, it's all pretty much downhill from here. At least that's what I thought. For some deranged reason, I assumed that once you got the kid walking, your parental responsibilities would slowly but surely taper off and you could return to going to the movies, hanging out with friends, and sleeping in. Needless to say, I was sadly, badly mistaken. Once the Precious Bundle starts to walk, all hell breaks loose. First of all, she won't stay where you put her. What's that all about? And you have to watch her every single second because she will try to kill herself about forty-five times a day. And then there's the fact that your baby will start to talk. I couldn't wait for Lulu to talk. I was constantly babbling away to her, but I never actually believed she would learn to respond. Those were the days. Now that I'm the mother of a very sassy twelve-year-old, "talking back" has a whole new meaning. But at the time, I thought I'd never tire of hearing that darling little voice.

The following Fifteen Guiding Lights will help you navigate the collision course of love, worry, and growth that's just around the corner.

RULE #87:
Write it down.

When you first hear those mangled little words, spoken with the sweetest little lisp, you think you'll never forget a single one. You will. I tried to write down all the adorable permutations of language that Lulu served up and to a great extent, I got them down. I just don't remember where I put them. So do yourself a favor and write the cutie-pie words on a piece of paper and immediately attach those scraps to her baby book. That way you won't be looking for all those darling malapropisms (like some people we know) for the next ten years. Or take a movie—but kids have a perverse way of not saying what you want them to the minute the camera is rolling.

RULE #88:
Buy new underwear.

This is actually a chronic piece of advice (meaning you have to keep doing it on a regular basis), and it doesn't come from me, it comes from a darling young man with whom I once

Kristi's **Cutie-Pie Story**
(which she wrote down)

I was in Target, and my son was singing his favorite song, "Bingo." He had just learned it and so he sort of sang it in little fits and starts, over and over, the way little kids do. I was hard at work shopping and not really paying attention, when I heard him stop in a place he'd gotten stuck three or four times before: "B-I-N-G-O, B-I-N-G-O, B-I-N-G-O . . ." His voice trailed off uncertainly and I was waiting for him to remember what came next when suddenly, from way across the store, came the booming baritone of an anonymous shopper who apparently couldn't stand the tension a second longer. "And Bingo was his name-O!" the stranger hollered out. Colin looked at me, his eyes wide with awe, and whispered, "Was that the *farmer?*"

worked. He was talking about his own little wife, and he said her underwear was so ragtag and worn, he felt like he was sleeping with Auntie Em. (From *The Wizard of Oz*, kids.) Ouch! Right then and there, I swore nobody would ever get to say that about me. Complain as you will about my bad personality and appalling temper, at least nobody can accuse me of having unappealing bras and panties.

Right now, when you're getting out of your nursing bras and your stomach is (praise God) flattening out, it's time to get some lovely, lacy new things. I guarantee this is one purchase your husband won't begrudge you.

RULE #89:
Proof it to me.

Child-proofing your home to prevent a childhood injury is a time-honored tradition, and many folks enthusiastically embrace the concept. My hyper-organized sister-in-law, for instance, bought thousands of utility outlet covers so wherever she went, she could prevent her toddler from electrocuting himself by sticking his fingers in sockets. Not to be callous, but my guess is that if you actually did shove your fingers into a socket, you'd get a rather nasty shock, which would provide you with a compelling reason not to do so again. Suffering the natural consequences of your dumb actions was the old-fashioned approach to child-proofing your home that my parents rigorously followed.

My dad, for instance, kept turpentine in the basement for soaking his paintbrushes. The container he used was an old Hawaiian Punch juice can, which at some point, every single one of his eight children pulled down from the workbench, thereby spilling turpentine directly into his or her eyes. It was agony—but did my dad change cans to some nonfood product or possibly consider a cover? Of course not. The kids would learn. And truth be told, none of us ever pulled that stunt twice. In fact, I never went near Hawaiian Punch again.

Now naturally, you don't want to make your home a harrowing gauntlet of dangerous objects that threaten your child's safety, tempting though that may be on days when he won't nap or stop fussing. But I do think some parents go a tad overboard—removing every vase and photo frame for forty miles, taping up the side of every piece of furniture, and sealing every cabinet shut like a vault. I simply couldn't. I'm too selfish, I am lock-challenged, and I like my house too much to make it look like a padded and stripped insane asylum. Of course, I moved the stuff that Lulu was always going to grab, and I tried to clear a nice, wide path for her because she loved to climb over every reachable surface (and some that were completely, terrifyingly beyond her reach). But that's just me. The one tip I can give you is that kids will generally work around obstacles and learn what to avoid. The other tip is to have eight children, so if you lose one, it won't matter so much.

RULE #90:

Carry that load.

Once a baby starts walking, many people feel it's unnecessary and coddling to carry him anymore. Well, listen to this. In Bali, the kid's feet never touch the ground until he's four months old. Literally. For 105 days, a parent, aunt, uncle, brother, sister, or friend continuously carries the baby, because they believe that children come directly from God and they are too sacred to touch the earth. I love that. Because when you carry your baby, you get to hug her, she hugs you back, and all's right with the world. I hope I'm not going to shock anybody by this admission (my father-in-law was horrified, but luckily I'm sort of immune to disapproval), but I carried

Lulu pretty much whenever she wanted until she was seven years old. Yeah, I know it was indulgent, but I also knew that she was the only baby I was ever going to have, and if she wanted to act like a baby in that one little way, I was more than willing to indulge her, if just for the hugs. So knock yourself out. Who knows? You might be carrying the next Dalai Lama.

P.S. If you think this directly contradicts my hard-ass advice on making the baby sleep on his or her own, you're right. We all have our weaknesses, and being Lulu's sherpa was mine. If letting your baby sleep with you until he's seventeen is yours (like it was my friend Donna's and she raised a strapping, *straight*, hunky professional baseball catcher), feel free to utterly disregard anything I say. I'm not Dr. Phil—thank God—and you're the mom. End of discussion.

RULE #91:
Keep 'em napping.

One of my favorite theories about kids is this: I figure the only reason they live to adulthood is that they look so completely adorable and sweet when they're asleep, we can't possibly kill them for all their demonic misdeeds while awake. In the spirit of that insight, I suggest you encourage napping as long as humanly possible (although my husband has taken this to an impressive fifty-year extreme). For one thing, the baby's nap allows you at least forty-five minutes of personal time, during which you can rearrange your spice cabinet or read 1/80th of the Sunday *New York Times*. Naptime also results in a quiet house, which is a blessing in and of itself. Finally, a nap often transforms a whiny, belligerent toddler into an adorable pink-with-sleep darling whom you actually want to nurture. It's miraculous! So keep the napping going as long as possible. Kids need sleep. Parents need kids to sleep. Sweet dreams.

RULE #92:

Get back in that closet.

Every woman alive has clothes she should never wear again. Dowdy. Frumpy. Ten years out of style. Ill-fitting and gro-tesquely unflattering. We know it, but we can't bring ourselves to throw those clothes away because they were either expen-sive, they're ridiculously comfortable, or someone gave them to us and we don't want to hurt their feelings. Please. As a new mother, you must be ferocious and brave, and pluck out these daily temptations to look your worst.

In a strong and confident moment (like after two glasses of wine, or better still, with a ruthlessly honest friend), you must go through your closet like Sherman stormed through Georgia, declaring total war. Stop using the barometer of "If I haven't worn it in a year, I'll get rid of it." You're trying to get rid of the bad stuff you unfortunately *do* wear, but shouldn't.

Use this barometer instead: Ask yourself, "Do I want to be seen in this? Is this how I want people to remember me?

Would I be happy to be wearing this if I bumped into that adorable UPS guy who is always giving me the once-over?" If the answer is "God, no!" then give it the heave-ho. I guarantee you'll instantly improve your fashion profile, and definitely get all your packages delivered, pronto.

RULE #93:
Rock your sole.
Right now, you'll see a lot of kids in adorable shoes: Reeboks, Nikes, Prada cross-trainers, shiny patent-leather Mary Janes, and golden Timberland boots. Resist the urge to join the parade. What kids need right now is no shoes at all. Instead, buy a couple pair of cute, rubber-bottomed, soft fabric booties that give your baby traction, without the constriction that is really bad for her feet, arches, and ankles. With all the action she's seeing, your baby will work her way through these puppies faster than you can get to the store again, hence the directive to buy more than one pair. Don't lace her up in stuff that's going to smother her footloose spirit. You'll have plenty of time for that later.

Of course, it's never too early to foster an enthusiastic attitude toward shoe shopping in general. So take her with you to the nearest Jimmy Choo or DWS store, solemnly explain the appeal of the four-inch stiletto, and let her watch you gulp when you hand over your credit card for those Dolce & Gabbana shoes you simply could not resist. This is what role modeling is all about!

RULE #94:
Just say no.

No is one of the all-time great words in the English language. It's so short, so all-purpose, so definite, so unambiguous. Then why is *No* getting such a bad rap? I have no idea!

Some friends of mine came to visit from Florida for about a month—or maybe it was just three days—with their fourteen-month-old child. About two hours into the visit, the darling boy started punching the buttons on my phone, causing it to leap into speaker mode with an ear-splitting screech and agonizing buzz. I watched him do this about a dozen times. Each time, his parents would gently remove his hands and turn the speaker off, only to have him pause dramatically until his parents' backs were turned, then lunge for the button again. Finally, I couldn't stand another round of the game, and employed the infamous N-word. Looking right into his cute little face, his sturdy little shoulders in my hands, I said calmly, "No, you may not touch that button. It's too loud. *No.*" He looked at me like he'd never heard the word before. Turns out he hadn't. His mother frostily informed me that she never uses the word because "it's so negative" and apparently children hear it, to chilling negative consequence, far too often in their fragile, developing little lives.

Give me a break. I love the word *No*. And so do kids. Your child, in a matter of months, is going to develop his own love affair with *No*—whether he's been shielded from its negative influence or not. So get over it. Simple clarity and easy-to-understand boundaries are surely preferable to some gauzy, affirmative no man's land where the kid doesn't know where the limits are, and what he is or isn't allowed to do. One thing I know for sure: The more negotiable the discussion, the more trouble you're in for when it comes to disciplining your Precious Bundle. (Discipline actually means "to teach," in case you think I'm being just a tad too punitive.) Anyhow, you're going to hear it enough coming back at you, so you might as well teach your child the true meaning of the word *No*. So he understands the power and the glory of the word.

RULE #95:
Beware the Internet.

I'm not taking about the dangerous effects of the Internet on our children—there's already more than enough parental angst for me to join the chorus. Nope, I'm talking about exerting some parental control over yourself. Speaking from painful personal experience, I know that e-mail alone can easily chew up four hours of your precious day, every day, before you realize that it's even happening. Don't believe me? E-mail me on my Web site (*www.toosexyformyvolvo.com*) and I'll bet I e-mail you back within thirty minutes. It's a pathetic addiction.

If this is how you want to spend your life, okay. But don't get in the habit of sending out 4,000 e-mail lucky chains, sweet thoughts, friendship notes, inspirational messages, and nudnik time-wasters just because somebody is bored enough to send them to you. Break the chain. Log off. Take a walk.

You don't want to look like you've got nothing better to do. Do you?

RULE #96:
Ditch the downers.

Because you're a new mom, chances are good that you've made some new friends lately, from the playground, day care, or the neighborhood. But friends, like diamonds (my other reason to live), come in all grades of quality. Some will make you feel like a million bucks—rich, indulged, and beloved—and some will make you feel cheesy, ridiculous, and vulnerable. It's a wise woman who keeps the gems and chucks the cubic zirconia. Nothing can bring you down faster than a bad friend—not even a bad lover. Men seem unable to help behaving badly, but when a woman betrays your trust, it's personal.

So, how do you recognize a bad friend? If you invariably feel lousy about yourself after every encounter, you need to pull the plug on the friendship. I mean this literally.

One former friend of mine would always find a way to tell me something bad that someone had said about me—or far worse, about Lulu—and I'd leave every rendezvous with her filled with anxiety. Of course, she always passed along the information under the guise of "I need to tell you something before you hear it from somebody else . . . " but the truth is, she couldn't wait to tell me hurtful things. When I finally decided not to invest any more time in the friendship, I felt like a twenty-pound weight fell off my neck. Friends like these are toxic.

Invest your friendship energy in shiny, happy people who support you, build you up, think you're fabulous, and see you the way you want to be seen. This does not mean to avoid women who are in a bad place or having trouble. It means avoid friends who *are* trouble.

And stop wasting time on people who don't bring something positive to the party.

RULE #97:
Consider an exciting future in modeling.

Okay, this is the part of the book where I tell you how difficult life can be, even when you're super thin and terribly beautiful and internationally famous and fabulously wealthy, because you really won't be able to trust anybody since all they want to do is to sleep with you. (Oops, no . . . that's my *next* book.)

Actually, this is the place where we talk about the word that first struck terror into my heart as Lulu became a lulu. Modeling, as in *behavior*. As in, your kid is probably going to be a lot like you in all the ways you wish to God she wouldn't, because you taught her by your *example*. Yep, she's going to learn kindness by listening to you curse at the idiot drivers randomly cutting into your lane with nary a thought of using their turn indicator. She's going to learn sweetness by hearing your phone conversation with Mimi, critiquing—Was it a caftan? Or a *bedspread?*—that what's-her-name was wearing to book club last night. She's going to learn patience by watching you lose your temper when she loses her winter jacket . . . for the fourth time. She's going to learn honesty by watching you lie to get her into the amusement park as a kid when she's really old enough to pay the adult admission.

I don't know what to tell you, except that everything they say about modeling is probably true, and I can keep myself awake for hours at night dreading it with all my heart, wishing I were a better person. Can it really be possible that Lulu will inherit every single one of my bad habits and none of that good one? At this point, I usually get up, throw cold water on my face, and realize it ain't happening. Of course I'm always going to feel the nagging insecurity that the kids are watching me and doing everything I do, like some weird pod creatures from another planet. Then I realize I can't even get them to put the cap on the toothpaste, and I've been modeling that behavior like crazy since the moment they entered my life. So give it up. Fear of modeling can only torture you and cause you to lose even more sleep—and you're already thousands of hours behind.

RULE #98:
Turn it off.

That would be television. And I bet you think I'm going to harsh out on television right about now, making all the normal people reading this feel like great big losers. Well, you're only half-right. I would be the worst kind of hypocrite (is there any other kind?) if I were to tell you that I never let Lulu near TV. How else was I going to get her to eat her breakfast every morning, while I ran upstairs to get dressed? Lulu and I were Disney junkies. We didn't watch TV much, but we did watch videos: *Dumbo, Bambi, Little Mermaid, Jungle Book, Beauty and the Beast, Lady and the Tramp, Charlotte's Web, The Swan Princess,* and *The Secret Garden,* plus all the original *Winnie the Pooh* tapes. We'd watch them over and over—we knew all the songs and all the characters; it was great. The only problem is that Lulu still adores television, movies, videos, and anything that doesn't involve reading, while I really can't stand TV. Too bad it's also my vocation. I hate TV; I watch TV. I hate TV commercials; I write TV commercials. How conflicted can one person be?

But wait, it gets worse! Once upon a time, I had Lulu in a Waldorf school. She was four, and it was the best preschool on the planet as far as I was concerned. Her teachers were soft-spoken and gentle, they wore skirts and floated around the classroom, made immense amounts of eye contact, and sang to the kids if they did something wrong. (Not exactly a staple form of discipline—I mean *teaching*—in our household.) All the toys in the classroom were handmade and exceptionally clever, and the children created amazing arts and crafts, even learning to sew, cook, and julienne vegetables. The teachers had wonderful harvest and solstice festivals and gave the kids back rubs at naptime. It was like a Baby Canyon Ranch, except with more tofu. I loved it. But the Waldorf ethos concerning popular culture is *intense*, which I found out the hard way.

At the first parent get-together, I came directly from work, wearing high-heeled black boots and a black leather jacket. In that environment of earthy moms in Birkenstocks and boiled wool socks, I looked like a Harley-Davidson hooker. Luckily, I was just in time for the conversation about TV. As I said, I am hardly an advocate of television—just because my career revolves around it doesn't mean I'm not keenly aware of how stupid, manipulative, and unrewarding a medium it can be. But these people were *out there.*

Okay, I probably asked for it. I made the gargantuan mistake of asking how other people coped with their children's desire to watch TV, since I believed my stern rationing of TV time was actually causing Lulu to value it more. Not so!

"It's really simple," one mom said, earnestly clasping the hand of her husband, who beamed proudly, nodding enthusiastically at me. "We just gave away our TV, and that's it. We don't have it, so we don't watch it. And our three kids don't even know who the Disney characters are!"

"That's right!" piped up another father, bedecked in fleece and a floral baby backpack. "We had a Turn It Off celebration and threw our television in the dumpster. The kids knew just where we were coming from!"

"In their hearts, they know they're not really missing anything," chimed in another recovering TV viewer with huge, sincere eyes and a dark braid down her back. "I think they're actually glad we've removed the temptation to watch it."

I was thinking about Lulu and envisioning her calm acceptance of the end of TV in our lives. Somehow I couldn't get there.

And in fact, I didn't want to. Like it or not, television *is* our culture. And despite the fact that I think television is an elixir that needs to be doled out in small doses and with great care, I also believe that to deprive yourself of it entirely is to take yourself out of the culture—and isn't that how that Guyana thing started? In the meeting, I slunk further and further into my seat as the helpful Waldorf crowd tried mightily to aid in my redemption—but I was, after all, in advertising *and* wearing animal products—and clearly, there was only so much they could do.

That was a defining moment for me. I knew I was never going to ban TV in my house, but I also knew that I had to find my own way. Now of course, the American Academy of Pediatrics has come out pretty strongly against TV—advising parents that *no TV at all* is the way to go from birth to age two. But I'll bet none of them follow through with that dictum in the privacy of their own dens. Why? Because it's damned inconvenient, for one thing. When a kid is watching TV, a kid is not complaining, and some days you really, really need that. However vigilant you try to be, kids are also going to watch TV at day care, at friends' homes, and in their *pediatrician's office*, for godsakes. And finally, the little darlings are going to wheedle and whine and fuss for TV until you can't stand it one single moment more. (Unless you go postal and throw your set entirely away, which is also punishing yourself.)

My policy with TV is one of containment. I believe you can start *right now* to get your child used to a little bit of television, and also get him used to the television being turned off.

I believe in television as a destination—watching a specific show or movie—not as an open buffet. And I believe in certain inalienable rules, such as no TV on weekdays, one hour of TV on weekend mornings, and lots and lots of outdoor time. My kids grouse about it all the time, but they know the rules and at least it's not a constant negotiation.

So do whatever feels right with TV—but remember, it doesn't have to be an either/or situation. Don't throw in the towel when you can just throw in a washcloth.

joy's to rule

This whole complex television negotiation has to work for you and for your kids in the real world, not in some fantasyland populated by saintly moms and understanding children. And it has to take into consideration that everybody needs a break sometimes. Don't get trapped into thinking TV is the single thing that's going to make or break your child's intellectual future. Relax. Treat yourself and your child to a little TV, call it bonding, and everyone will applaud you for it. At least I will.

RULE #99:
Shine on.

I may not know precisely how to preserve your fabulosity, but I definitely know how to kill it. And that is to allow your entire life to revolve around your child's "needs." In fact, a baby has very few needs—but one of the most important is the need for a schedule. Remember Copernicus and his revolutionary

Random **Acts** of **Selfishness**

Ten entirely acceptable ways to *not* be a mother who gives too much.

1. Don't answer the phone.
2. Don't fold the laundry.
3. Do take baths.
4. Do buy thick, beautiful stationery.
5. Do eat the last cookie.
6. Don't reward yourself with food.
7. Do go to the movies.
8. Do buy good workout clothes.
9. Don't scrimp on your hair.
10. Do buy flowers.

discovery? The sun does not revolve around the earth; the earth revolves around the sun. And you, my dear, are the sun. The baby simply thinks he is the sun because of his perspective, but it is your sacred responsibility not to send him out into the world with this delusion (lest he become somebody else's Mr. Wrong). This means that starting right now, the baby needs to sleep on a fairly regular schedule, not whenever he decides to. The baby needs to eat on a schedule, which means that you offer him food at a regular time (not that he will always eat it). And the baby needs to learn to sublimate his whims and his desire to control the universe to yours, not vice versa. This is not cruelty. This is called parenting.

Listen up. There is literally no way you can ever get back to your exciting, dazzling, fascinating self if your time, attention, destiny, and every waking hour are consumed with the demands of your darling child. Be strong. Be the sun.

RULE #100:
Be thankful.

The day your baby celebrates her first birthday is a very special day. You've made it through the first year! In many countries in this world, one in five babies won't live to see their first birthday, so you have plenty of cause to rejoice. Take this day to be truly grateful for the gift of life you've received, and the 365¼ days you've gotten to spend with your own little angel. Get out your glad rags and celebrate what a fabulous mom you are and what an undeniably gorgeous pair the two of you make. (And don't forget to get it on film.)

ginger's birthday rant

I hate birthday parties. Especially birthday parties in this age of overkill. My parents used to have one-hour birthday parties for each of us eleven kids—our friends would come over, eat cake, open presents, run around outside, and go home. For party favors, my parents would throw handfuls of peanuts on the ground, and we'd all fall on them like a pack of dogs. It was great!

Today you're expected to put together a four-hour extravaganza at a dazzling venue, with entertainment, serious food, and my personal nemesis: loot bags. What's that all about? You spend $100 on crap the kids throw in the back of their closet the nanosecond they get home. People have even written *books* on how to throw a kid's birthday party. It's not like this is the secret to a happy childhood, people. Keep it simple. Keep it short. Keep your sanity. (And I only let my kids have a birthday party every other year. Don't report me!)

RULE#101:
Make your own play dates.

As overscheduled as our chidren's lives are, a mom's life can be pathetically underscheduled . . . for fun. In order to have fun, you have to *commit* to fun. You have to seek out fun. And you have to show up for fun. This means you've got to take some *action*. Join a book club. Go to a museum you've always wanted to see. Take a road trip someplace that intrigues you. Plan a progressive dinner with friends. Go out late for cocktails with your husband, after the babe is in bed and before you collapse in front of the TV. Browse in a bookstore and buy a book you'd never ordinarily read. Order dinner in and serve it on your prettiest china. Go for a hike someplace wild. Don't wait for anybody to join you; go alone if you have to. Take time for yourself, to celebrate and recon-nect with your awesome Inner Babe—the one who existed before motherhood. She's still in there. So get out there. Be creative. Go wild. Be fabulous.

Bonus Pointer for Domestic Goddesses:
Protect your boundaries.
When you don't work outside the home, it's easy for working moms (if they are totally unconscious) to assume that you're available for free childcare. Sometimes this arrangement can work out happily, and you will feel appreciated, reimbursed, and treasured for your generosity. But sometimes this arrangement will result in your feeling manipulated and used, like domestic roadkill. It is your duty to establish boundaries and not allow working mothers to trespass across them. Unless you really do fancy yourself Joan of Arc or you are being duly compensated, do not volunteer to watch other people's children if they get sick, if mom gets stuck at an impromptu cocktail party, or if dad has to suddenly leave for Cleveland. If neighborhood children randomly drop by and stay for hours, send them home. Even if your children are being entertained and enjoy the other children being around, unless you feel comfortable with the situation and you're certain it won't escalate into you providing full-time day care, end it.

Establishing your boundaries doesn't even require a conversation or confrontation. If it really isn't something you want to do, simply say, "I'm sorry I'm not able to help," and if the boxcar children have a tendency to just show up on your doorstep, tell them you have other plans for the day. Be firm about this. Your entire little kingdom is at stake.

CHAPTER NINE

The Far Beyond: Years 1 to 20

when does it get easy?

i t never gets easy. But sometimes it does get easier. It did for me. Astonishingly, I do have a happy ending for this story. (You weren't expecting that now, were you?) Yes, after four years of hopeless and pathetic attempts to land the unlandable Mr. Wrong, he finally proposed. We were engaged. He bought me a ring. However, I quickly realized that a few wedding bells were not going to herald the end of Mr. Wrong's big runaround. No, the bells would toll only for me. At the same time that I had that blindingly obvious revelation, I also—miraculously—became attracted to someone else. Someone young and beautiful. An adorable man who clearly adored me. Someone—unmiraculously—married. Oh well.

Predictably, at my first halfhearted, faint-hearted foray into infidelity, Mr. Wrong freaked out. Lost his mind with jealousy. Was almost hospitalized for a near-total loss of equilibrium. (Of course, he continued to date, while racking his brain over how to win me back, which was almost heroic in its hypocrisy.) And then, finally, it was over. I was free. I was alone. And I was sure, certain, adamantly positive I would never meet anyone again. Ever.

I slunk back to my high-school reunion—only because I was going to be East for a family reunion, and I had no excuse not to go. And there I re-met Lawrence, a nice Jewish boy turned extremely handsome and accomplished Jewish man, whom I've known since junior high Latin class. He had three young kids, a gorgeous body, a huge brain, a real job, and a substantial house. Three months later, we got married.

We're still married. We have raucous sex every night, never fight, are raising four perfect kids who all get along, and have gobs of money.

Okay, it's not *exactly* that kind of happy ending.

Some days we can't stand the sight of each other; other days I'm so filled with gratitude for our life together that it takes my breath away. Our kids are wonderful—and it's a near-constant agony trying to make sure they're happy, healthy, and growing up well. The struggle to create harmony in a blended household is Herculean and, on the few days it works, positively elating. In short, our lives are probably a lot like everybody else's. And the longer I'm a mother, the more I love it and the harder it gets—with the ultimate hardness, of course, looming ahead: the prospect of having to let my sweet little girl go. Whatever the peculiar and unique geography of your life, you've got plenty to look forward to along the way. Here's a glimpse: Ten Far Beyond (FaB) Insights into the heart and soul of motherhood.

FaB RULE #1:
Quality time is an oxymoron.
Let's get one thing clear. There is no such thing as quality time. There is only quantity time. Sometimes the quantity time you spend with your child will be of good quality and sometimes it will be of lousy, painstaking, and truly annoying quality.

The myth that you can plan to have meaningful, mutually rewarding little snippets of time with your child—at your convenience, of course—is as laughable as the idea that your schedule and priorities are going to remain sacrosanct in this great adventure we call parenting. Did I not mention that your child will gobble up huge chunks of your life, without so much as a backward glance? The fact is, once you have a child, your life is not your own—you're sharing it with him. (That and your money, your entire CD collection, and all your bathroom amenities.) Of course, the more quantity time you spend with your child, the more quality time you will have— simply because the achingly sweet moments in which your child reveals himself to you can and will happen at the most unpredictable times: Driving to the store to return a hideous birthday sweater. Waking up from a nap together. Getting stuck in an airport. In fact—predictably—the "fun" quality time that's been planned for months can often end up horribly disappointing, while the 102-degree fever that forces you to take off from work leads to a day of cuddling, reading, and nonstop affection. Go figure. One thing I can promise you: If you're only in it for the quality time, you'll get less and less of it as the years go by. Spend the time. Reap the rewards.

FaB RULE #2:
Four-year-olds are supposed to do that.

As a mother, I am a notoriously slow learner. For instance, I didn't really get the concept of age-appropriate behavior until Lulu was four. It was a moment of blasting enlightenment. I was at my shrink's office, running through a dire litany of Lulu's behavior felonies, when she said calmly to me, "Well, she's supposed to do all that. It's entirely age-appropriate." When I gaped at her in obvious disbelief, she suggested I look into a comprehensive series of books focused on age-appropriate behavior, specifically *Your Four-Year-Old: Wild and Wonderful*.

I was desperate, so that night I went directly out to the bookstore to pick up a copy. When I approached the elaborate Parenting section, I immediately saw the series, with every year fully stocked and colorfully displayed. Except for *Your Four-Year-Old*. It was completely sold out. Back-ordered, in fact. That made me feel so good—obviously, at least a few other parents felt similarly inept, clueless, and furious at their Wild and Wonderful four-year-olds—that I went home and poured myself a nice, big, restorative glass of Merlot.

Age-appropriate behavior can either be the world's biggest cop-out or a parental lifeline. It's not meant to excuse vile behavior or justify parental irresponsibility (except in my case). But it can definitely help you understand that when your two-year-old insists upon flinging herself off the top bunk and onto the air mattress below, seventy-five times in a row, it is not necessarily a sign that you should immediately reserve space for her in the juvenile delinquent hall, but merely something many kids do at this age. This information can be immensely helpful to an anxiety-ridden parent who is struggling to cope with a headstrong, precocious child, particularly at her family reunion when everyone else's kid is being peachy keen, serenely charming, and revoltingly well-behaved and yours is—well, methodically throwing herself off bunk beds.

Chances are, your friends and family will not be able to help you with words of wisdom on age-appropriate behavior because of a weird quirk of nature known as Parental Amnesia, which manifests itself like this: The minute your kids grow out of one stage, you instantly and permanently forget what that stage was really like, making you far more willing to re-reproduce and go through it all again. An example: A few years ago I went back to visit my friend Clarice in Colorado, and her four-year-old drove me crazy. He insisted upon going with us on our walks. He insisted upon going with us to the mall. He insisted upon going with us to the movies. He was whiny. So clingy. So prone to tantrums and bouts of crying. How did Clarice stand it? Once I got home, I was looking through some old papers and found my diary from when Lulu was four. She was so insistent upon going everywhere with me. So whiny. So clingy. So nasty and confrontational. Whoops!

It's just age-appropriate stuff. Educate yourself. It can truly save your sanity and make you a more compassionate mother.

remy's worst-case-scenario rule
When all else fails and you're feeling like a totally crap mother, lower the bar. Seriously. Go find books on the *Mommie Dearest* theme, rent the movie *Mermaids,* or better still, some foreign film in which mothers routinely *sell* their children. Then use this as your yardstick. Why measure yourself against paragons of virtue when you can measure yourself against someone who conclusively proves you are not the worst mother on the planet? Sure it's stacking the deck, but who cares? Your kids hold all the cards anyhow.

FaB RULE #3:
Shut your eyes and drive.

It's sort of flattering—but mostly frightening—when somebody plays back, verbatim, memorable things that you said years (or a few weeks) ago, which you have absolutely no recollection of saying at all. That happens to me a lot, which is either a sign of early Alzheimer's, or . . . something else. In any event, "Shut your eyes and drive" was apparently a Betty *bon mot* I used to describe my somewhat reckless approach to life in my twenties, recollected by my dear friend Kate.

I am hereby resurrecting "Shut your eyes and drive" for all you daughters of perfect mothers, a club of which I consider myself to be a charter member. Seriously. My mother never drank or smoked. She was gentle and kind. She was brilliant and compassionate. She was modest and religious. She was optimistic and happy. She was even-tempered and infinitely patient, never raising so much as her voice, while she raised all eight of us kids.

Okay, so imagine you are the foul-mouthed, evil-tempered, high-strung, self-centered, hypercritical, and wickedly volatile daughter of such perfection. What in the world would possess you to attempt to follow in those formidable maternal footsteps? Nothing! Hence, my directive: *Shut your eyes and drive.*

You won't be *your* mother (except in ways that truly frighten and disturb you). But you will be *a* mother, which in my humble opinion is a heck of a lot better than sitting on the parental sidelines waiting for your personality to improve. The good news is, you're the only mother your child will have. Which means you will be the norm, no matter how abnormal you actually are! The only one making specious comparisons in which you come out looking bad is—you guessed it—you. (And maybe a sister or two.)

The next two Rules are a tribute to my mother, representing just a few tricks from her astonishing and encyclopedic book of mom-dom.

FaB RULE #4:
Take it outside.

My mother passionately believed that the great outdoors was the cure for boredom, depression, raging hormones, anxiety, a listless sinus system, and sibling rivalry. Consequently, we slept with the windows cracked open (in winter, in Buffalo), we were all sent outdoors to play at least once a day (basically from sunrise till sunset), and we all developed ridiculously robust immune systems and very wide feet (from running around barefoot for three months every summer). Nowadays, of course, thanks to the ubiquitous Milk Carton Alert, parents naturally assume that an unsavory character is lurking around every corner, hoping to abduct their child. (For an antidote, read "The Ransom of Red Chief," a short story by O. Henry. The soothing premise is—let's be honest—who would want your kid?) Nowadays people keep their kids safe indoors, where they can play violent video games and watch sex-drenched MTV all day long. Gone are those long, adventure-packed afternoons spent playing by a (dangerous) creek, romping around in the (poisonous, pedophile-infested) woods, climbing (perilously high) trees, and playing (competitive, bone-shattering) block games. What a loss! Even to ride a bike, today's kids have to gear up like they're preparing to scale Everest. Granted, it's great to keep your child safe and under supervision. But kids also need to run around, get into some mischief, and scoot out from beneath the watchful eyes of their parents and into the wild. Your child's imagination will be better stimulated by climbing a rock pile, capturing fireflies in a bottle, and lying on his back in the grass looking up at the clouds than by any educational video on the planet. As an added bonus, if your kids learn the love of the outdoors, you won't have to work so hard to make your internal environment do all the heavy lifting of entertaining them. Remember that old business school adage: *Keep it simple, stupid?* It's not such a dumb approach to parenting, either. Send 'em outdoors and let 'em play.

FaB RULE #5:
Picnic is a verb.

Every time she got the chance, my mother would bundle us kids into the car and head out on a picnic. If it was cold and rainy, that just made it more of an adventure. She would tie her plastic rain cap firmly under her chin, caution us to look for a spot under some trees to prevent the sandwiches from getting soggy, then encourage us to run around to build up our appetites. My father hated the great outdoors so he usually stayed at home, risking her wrath by smoking cigars and watching auto racing on TV. But we kids never dreamed of saying no. For one thing, food was involved. For another, our picnics were totally fun. We ran around like maniacs, played in the woods, jumped from stone to stone over creeks till our legs were trembling with fatigue, and invented all kinds of ferociously competitive games. I can vividly recall every aspect of our picnicking gear: the weathered wooden picnic basket; dented aluminum thermos: sturdy tin cups in rainbow colors; thick, marbleized three-section plates; and battered old mother-of-pearl utensils, all placed on top of a creased, faded red oilcloth backed with felt that my mother would wipe down carefully before putting it on top of the old, dirty wooden picnic tables in the park of the day.

Eating outdoors is a gas. For one thing, you don't really have to cook, you certainly don't have to clean up like you do inside, and if you make it an outing, your kids will love it. Now that I've experienced the deep satisfaction of cooking for a passel of vicious food critics (also known as my children), I realize that all those picnics were probably just my mother's way of getting out of the stupid kitchen and making sandwiches into a meal, but who cares what the motivation is? This is not Method Acting; it's trying to get through a meal without going nuts. Make it alfresco and chill.

FaB RULE #6:
Choosing the right preschool
(and other anxiety attacks).

This may be a tad premature. But sooner or later, you're going to be in the position of choosing a school for your Precious Bundle. For some, this may be a clear-cut decision, made quickly and efficiently with little fuss or bother. For others, it will take on all the emotional freight and psychological baggage of a season of *The Sopranos*. I sincerely hope for your sake you're in the snappy, decisive first group, but in the event you find yourself like me, mired in the morass of incessant school insecurity, here are a few words of wisdom.

First, don't send your child to any school that feels weird to you, no matter how highly recommended it is. For one year, I sent my little Lulu to a well-regarded Lutheran school in Denver (I thought Lutherans were sort of like Catholics Lite—boy, was I mistaken!) and I've never forgiven myself. I should have yanked her out the first time they described the crucifixion in gory, revolting detail to the wide-eyed little three-year-olds. They kept sending home notes complaining that Lulu danced too much in the classroom and was laughing too much in the library. And she wouldn't "walk on the rope." (They expected all the children to walk through the halls, to lunch, and to recess hanging onto big hairy knots in a giant rope.) The whole episode still makes me want to cry.

Second, don't stop at rejection. If you really want your child to get into a certain school, be relentless. Butter up anybody who could possibly matter. Charm the living daylights out of the admissions office. Show up at every meeting, every volunteer opportunity, every parent orientation. Work any connection you have at the school—teachers, development folks, board members, donors. Leave no stone unturned. Listen, that's the way the world works. So work it for your child.

Third, don't get too nuts. I have been guilty of relentlessly agonizing over Lulu's schools for as long as I can remember, and all it's gotten me is a brooding suspicion that I missed the point. Fact is, there is no perfect school for your child, but many options that could work. The less you make it a case of pass/fail for *you*, and a case of what's right for her at that moment in time, the better off you're going to be. As my lovely friend Toni, who taught in both public and private schools in Denver and raised three lovely, successful kids once told me, "The only thing I can say for sure about public versus private schools is this: good students do well in school." See? It's a crapshoot, and there are no answers.

But this is truly my Achilles' heel, so shame on me for writing as if I bring any wisdom to the subject. I just thought I'd let you know that however deranged this topic makes you, you've got company in the padded cell.

FaB RULE #7:
Rant on.

Somewhere during the first few years of trying to create the perfect Blended Family (sounds like a new Chinese entrée, doesn't it?) my amazingly telepathic friend Michelle sent me an article by Harriet Lerner on being a stepparent. To paraphrase, it said there are three things you need to know about being a stepmother: First, it's very hard. Second, it's really, really difficult. Third, it's much harder than anyone can possibly imagine. I cut out that article and saved it for years—because the mere acknowledgment of the difficulty of what I was attempting to do was like manna from heaven.

Misery doesn't love company. Misery loves *recognition*.

Even today, with my fabulous faithful husband and gorgeous kids, I'm still selfish and ungrateful enough to want to hear some other sweet mother admit, "Yes, I, too, am frequently tempted to torch my house and run away with a motorcycle gang. More coffee??"

Now, there's a fine line between being heard and understood and just ranting until you get totally worked up for no purpose. I have no idea where that line is, but I suspect I cross it on a fairly regular basis. However, I still believe it's better to get that rancor out than to bottle it up inside, trying to be perfect. (It's all the people around me who would love it if, just for once, I would put a cork in it—but that's not likely to happen any time soon.) Don't be too long-suffering. Express yourself. Rant a little. Then pick up your copy of *Don't Sweat the Small Stuff*, draw yourself a mammoth fragrant bath, and be serene.

suzette's ZZ Top rule

When I get too frustrated and angry to even try to talk, I'll just pull out a CD with a lot of energy, like Gipsy Kings or ZZ Top or Madonna, and blast it. Then I dance around the room until I'm dripping with sweat, and I can't be that mad any more. At least instead of hollering at the kids, I'm doing something productive, like burning calories. When my kids hear the music blaring, they've learned to cut me a wide berth, which is exactly what I need. And my husband just heads directly out and buys flowers. Smart man.

FaB RULE #8:
It's supposed to be hard.

Some days parenting is as deep and profound a joy as anything in life. Other days it's like breaking rocks. Difficult. Grinding. And thankless.

Even before I heard the story about Nelson Mandela, the phrase *It's like breaking rocks* had a poignant twang to it. Now, it haunts me. When Nelson Mandela was imprisoned in South Africa for almost twenty-seven years, the authorities made him and the other inmates break huge boulders of rock into small pieces, until those stone fragments could fit through a ring the size of an orange. All the while they were doing this backbreaking labor, the men figured they were making rocks for roads, and this small sense of accomplishment ennobled their work and gave it purpose—until the guards pointed out to the inmates that the tons and tons of orange-sized rocks they had produced were simply taken out into the harbor and dumped.

The difference is, unlike Nelson Mandela's heartbreaking tale, even the times when motherhood feels like breaking rocks (and there will be more days like that than you can imagine), it is still about building something important: Your little person. Try to hold on to that. And hang in there. Being

Michel's Small Comfort

Parenting can be incredibly difficult, but every once in a while you get this transcendent moment of pure joy—and for me, this was one. I was on a trip with my son, who was taking his first flight on an airplane. We took off and he was holding my hand tightly, with his nose pressed up against the window, staring at the earth receding away from us below. "Hey Dad," he asked me in a hushed little voice, "when do we start getting small?"

I figure that moment will get me pretty much through his whole adolescence.

a parent is bloody hard work, and there's no guarantee of happiness or ease. But tomorrow might be one of those glorious days when the Precious Bundle is chirpy and content, you're relaxed and loving, no one says a harsh word, and you all go to sleep happy. Envision that. Because literally before you know it, your mommy days will be drawing to a close and you'll wish with all your heart that you could go back and live it all over again.

FaB RULE #9:
Learn to let go.

Since it first occurred to me (in the maternity wing) that this precious child of mine would eventually grow up and move away, I've been grieving in advance. Why waste time living in the present? Of course, if current trends continue, by the time the fateful day of separation does arrive, Lulu may have become so unpleasant and so openly disdainful of my company, I will be more than willing to let her go. But don't count on it.

She just takes up so much of my mind, my heart, and my time—all of which I give willingly and eagerly—I can't imagine what is going to come in and replace that. Gardening? Environmental activism? Chronic infidelity? (Just kidding, Larry.) I'm not talking about an empty nest here; I'm talking about a whole empty forest. That's how big and hollow it feels. In fact, I feel like throwing up just thinking about it. As I said, if and when I learn to let go, I'll let you know. That's the best I can offer.

FaB RULE #10:
Don't listen to me.

I am not a great mother. Some days I'm not even a very good mother. Which is one of the reasons I wrote this book. I felt it was high time that somebody who wasn't an expert—who wasn't, in fact, even particularly exemplary—talked about the pleasures and pain of being a mother. Somehow that seemed more real to me than listening to Berry Brazelton, bless his heart, remind me once again that it's important not to raise my voice at my little darling. I KNOW THAT! But the distance between knowing and being capable of modulating my voice when my offspring is being insufferably insolent is way, way behind the scope of my control. Does that make me an utter failure as a mother? Probably. However, with all of my multiple faults and flaws, being a mother is still my absolute greatest source of joy. Remember that old Peace Corps line, "The toughest job you'll ever love"? Well, that's how I feel about motherhood. I find the older the kids get, the harder it gets, but it never fails to be anything less than full-on compelling and to my mind, completely engrossing. I've never had anything I cared about more passionately, wanted to be good at more desperately, felt less competent to handle, and was more eager to sacrifice my life for.

The truly ironic twist is that in this, your most important job as a human being, you won't know if you've been successful or not for another two or three decades. The jury is so far out, it's in another zip code. And let's not forget, even when your kids are grown, they could still do something appalling,

Senseless Acts of Beauty

Ten ways to bring beauty into your world, and joy to yourself and others:

1. Grow something.
2. Buy art you love.
3. Make your own valentines.
4. Learn to bake bread.
5. Set a pretty table.
6. Read poetry.
7. Write down things that move you.
8. Surround yourself with beautiful fabrics.
9. Listen to music.
10. Fall in love with nature.

like leaving their spouse and children to run away with the kids' swim coach at age forty—which of course is going to be pretty much all your fault, too.

Cheer up. It only gets harder. And you only love the little monsters more. Welcome to life as a mother.

Soliloquies for Single Mothers

is anybody out there?

E veryone gets to the Single Mother destination by a different route. Some choose the sperm bank, some get widowed, some do the leaving, and some get left. As you know by now (if you haven't snoozed through this entire book), I took the canine path to single mommydom, in a portent of those immortal words, "If you lie down with dogs, you get up with fleas." I did lie down with a dog, and I got up with Lulu—which all things considered, was a brilliant tradeoff.

However you get there, being a single mother is a vastly underrated experience. I myself did not quite appreciate it at the time, but believe me when I tell you that the grass is not necessarily greener over here on the marital side of the fence. Sure, it's a bit easier when you've got the famous male authority figure to back you up, as you throw down the gauntlet with your two-year-old and growl, "I mean it, mister!" Carpooling is simpler, too. And usually there's a bit more money to go around. However, when you live with a man, chances are fairly good that he'll expect you to pay some attention to him, and that can take up a *lot* of time. Time that—let's face it—could sometimes be more enjoyably and productively spent painting your toenails, folding laundry, and watching the Lifetime Channel. Be that as it may, when you're a single mom, you've got a lot on your plate. Here are Fifteen Flying Solo Rules to help you wing your way through it with gusto and style.

SOLO RULE #1:
Think beyond the ring.

I was morally and politically okay about having a baby out of wedlock (I despise that term; it makes it sound like you're in prison if you're married, or like some parade you'll never be asked to join, if you're unwed). Despite my inner equanimity about being a single parent, I felt painfully exposed by the lack of gold on my third finger, left hand. It wasn't that I wanted to be married—well, actually, it *was* that I wanted to be married. And I felt that empty real estate on my finger was like a huge neon sign announcing to everyone that HE DIDN'T LOVE ME, which is particularly pathetic when you've got his love child strapped to your chest. If you don't like going public with the information that you're an unmarried mother, just get a ring and wear it.

I wasted a lot of time wandering through thickets of tortured logic: Was it more pitiful to wear a ring and pretend to be married when you weren't? Or to walk around with your diamond-free digit like a scarlet letter, proclaiming that you were Not Married? Finally, I just decided to wear my grandmother's big, wide wedding band on my middle finger, and though I doubt it convinced anyone, especially me, that I was somebody's beloved spouse, it did make me feel less exposed as an Unwed Mother. Which, for me, was a good thing.

SOLO RULE #2:
Make the most of being unconventional.

Okay, so you're not married. And you're pregnant. Well, that makes you, by choice or by chance, someone who's not exactly coloring inside the lines in the Great Activity Book of Life. And like me, you will probably encounter some level of disapproval or reprobation during your pregnancy and motherhood. All this is true. But for every action in the universe, there's an equal and opposite reaction. (That's not a Betty rule; it's Newton's Third Law of Motion.) And this law guarantees that, along with whatever social stigma you'll suffer for being such a rebel (you trollop!), you will also get the astonishing freedom that comes with it, just as sure as toast comes with that little plastic packet of jelly. In short, for the next nine months, you can get away with pretty much anything you want—and pregnant women are given a *lot* of slack anyhow, probably out of fear of those raging hormones. The good and bad news here is that you've got nobody to answer to but yourself. Your husband can't tell you what to name the kid, because *he's not there*. Your mother-in-law can't tell you that you've gained too much weight because *you don't have one*. Mommy gets to make all the decisions because *mommy is boss*. You don't have to feed somebody else, listen to anybody else, love, honor and obey anybody else, or even take anybody else's feelings into consideration when you're deciding where to live, what to eat, how to dress, or whether or not to shave your legs. It's your life to live, any way you want to live it. And that freedom is a fabulous gift.

Unwrap it.

SOLO RULE #3:
Name that Daddy.

Unless you're completely convinced that you are never going to want one thin dime of child support (and you've listened to friends and family who concur that this is a good position for you to take), do not let pride or prejudice overrule the logic of assigning parental rights to the papa. The father does not have to agree to be named, or be present to win. All you have to do is write his name on the appropriate line. If the father is around even temporarily, the sheer emotionality of the day of birth may induce him to take responsibility. If not (or if extenuating circumstances like surrogates, donor egg, or donor sperm complicate the situation), please get legal counsel beforehand.

Naming the father does not mean that you *have* to sue for child support; it simply means that you *can*—and for the good of your child, you should keep that option open. Another motivating nudge: if the dad should die, *in flagrante delicto*, for example, your baby would be eligible for his Social Security and have a claim on his estate, both of which would be time-consuming and complicated to prove without the birth certificate.

But wait, there's more!

Even if Dad is the biggest schmuck on the planet, *and* you believe he doesn't deserve to be named as parent of your amazing baby, *and* you're filthy rich and will never need child support at all, you *still* need to name the father. Every child has a right to know who both of his or her parents are. Getting it straight right from the start on the birth certificate is a fundamental responsibility you have to your darling offspring.

You're likely to be groggy, foggy, and out of it when they come around to get this information from you. Be prepared. Do the right thing.

SOLO RULE #4:
Something is not always better than nothing.
The last trimester of pregnancy can make you feel so vulnerable (see Rule #33), it's easy to delude yourself into thinking that you have to have a man by your side to get through it, no matter what kind of chowderhead the man in question actually is. This is not a healthy state of mind and can, in fact, lead you to accept far too little at the very time when you should be swimming in love and attention.

During the last few months before Lulu was born, I felt so desperate to extract a commitment from Mr. Wrong that I overlooked every signal he was trying to give me that he wasn't going to stick around. (Including the time he said cryptically, "I'm not going to stick around.") Instead of telling him to get lost, I managed to drag out the train wreck of our relationship in agonizing slow motion. I lent him big chunks of money. I gave him my car. I did his laundry, cooked for him, and watched his daughter while he went out at night. Had enough? Yeah, me too. It's painful to remember how pathetic I was, thinking that any scrap of a relationship with Mr. Wrong was better than nothing.

I wish now that I hadn't let his detachment taint the sweet days of my pregnancy, and that I had been brave enough to look at the facts and see that Mr. Wrong was never going to morph into Mr. Wonderful Father and Husband. Or even Mr. Remotely Acceptable Guy. Nope, he was going to stay Mr. Wrong forever—and if I had just been able to lie down with that, I could have spared myself and Lulu a lot of grief.

It's important that you hear me say this, girls. I could have made a *better* choice for my baby by ditching her dad when he clearly expressed his inability to make a commitment. Of course, that would have meant flying in the face of all the hormones and emotions that were flooding me with the feeling that I *must* not be alone and I *must* provide a father for my child. What I learned far later—and far more painfully—was that if you're happy (or even marginally stable), you will be far healthier and more successful as a single mother than if you muck around and let some guy make you mental.

There's nothing more to it.

SOLO RULE #5:
Cherish the simplicity of your life.

Whenever you feel overwhelmed and crabby about being a single mother (or if you never feel that way but just need to feel superior to someone), go over and visit another new mom who has been blessed with a husband. Preferably when the husband is there. Do not try to seduce the husband. Instead, simply and unobtrusively observe the household dynamic. See if the husband is contributing to the care and upkeep of Baby. See if the husband is contributing to the care and upkeep of Mommy. See if Mommy is competing with Daddy for parental rights to Baby. See if Mommy is spending enormous amounts of time, energy, and cheerleading to engage, manage, and motivate Daddy.

Then go home and take a nice, long nap with your own baby.

Now, don't you feel better? Of course, it's always preferable to have a two-parent household and that is truly nature's way, blah, blah, blah. But really? Sometimes it's far more exhausting having two people to worry about, particularly when one is an infant and the other just acts that way. I am quite certain

that there are a lot of men out there who are enormously helpful when it comes to parenting (well, maybe not *certain*), but
sometimes it comes down to the question of whether it's easier
to manage someone, or do the job yourself. Quite frankly,
there's a lot to be said for the sole proprietor approach to
motherhood. When you get married again you'll understand
exactly what I mean.

SOLO RULE #6:
Use bookmarks.
I love to read. And I loved reading to Lulu. But when she was
very small and I was very bummed that her father had left
us for about the fortieth time, reading stories to her about
families with a mommy, daddy, and baby was unbearable. It
seemed like I was only filling her head with something she was
never going to have. So I began a search for great kids' books
sans the nuclear family. Not books that made a big deal out
of our "special" status and how okay it is to be a single-parent
family (barf); just books that didn't relentlessly end up with
Daddy coming home and kissing Mommy and making everything okay.

Along the way to finding those books I loved, someone
gave me the very popular kids' book, *I Love You Forever*. It's
the tale of a mother with such a severe attachment disorder,
she spends a lifetime forcing her way into her son's house and
bedroom until he's in his late fifties, and she finally dies. All
I can remember is one truly disturbing illustration of the

Children's Books to Cure Your Queasiness

1. Fairy tales—These are great because they often feature orphans who are far, far worse off than your Precious Bundle will ever be . . . or better still, children with evil stepmothers—the classic enemy. (And I should know, because I've been on both sides of that great divide.) Goodness knows, there are enough fairy tales to last a childhood or two. And enough violence, dysfunction, and malevolence in those stories to satisfy the most bloodthirsty little cherub.
2. *Sesame Street*—Lots of single moms here, gritty urban living, and few discernable family units at all. Enchanting!
3. Animal stories, but beware: these can belabor the mommy/daddy theme, too.
4. A lot of the Little Golden Books, such as *The Pokey Little Puppy* and *The Little Yellow Taxi*; plus *Ping*, *Goodnight Moon* and *Pat the Bunny.*
5. Any books by Eric Carle or the incendiary and fabulous Maurice Sendak.
6. And of course, who could forget Ludwig Bemelmans's *Madeline*? The parents never show up and the kids are all happy as larks with Miss Clavel. Makes even medical emergencies like a ruptured appendix seem fun!

gray-haired "baby" in his pajamas snuggled up in his ancient mother's lap. Yeech!

And how about Shel Silverstein's *The Giving Tree*? A story of pure, masochistic love that ends up with the Giving Tree all tapped out and nothing but a stump, having given The Boy its fruit, leaves, bark, branches, and wood. Yet the plucky little stump is still happy it could provide a comfy place for the self-ish bastard to sit. I don't think so.

Don't trust the experts or the bestseller lists here. There's an entire School of Harrowing Children's Literature out there, but that doesn't mean you have to bring it home to your nurs-ery. If a book makes you squirm, honor that feeling. Read your child something *you* love.

SOLO RULE #7:
Language has power.

Maybe I'm too sensitive (fat chance), but I find the language aimed at single mothers to be an assault on the psyche. I couldn't find one single term for what I was, or what Lulu was, that didn't feel downright degrading. Let's go to the Thesaurus of Shame: "Broken home." "One-parent household." "Illegiti-mate." "Bastard." "Out of wedlock." "Unwed mother." "Love child." Ouch! Every word reeks of failure, while it neatly clas-sifies you or your child as an outsider.

I'm not sure what to do to rectify this situation, short of resorting to the New Age crap that beset the women's move-ment and resulted in torturously hyphenated last names and odd, mishmash titles like "waitrons" and "chairpersons." Spare me. Nevertheless, this is a topic that could bear some reflec-tion. If you start simply by recognizing the cruelty of the sub-text, you may be able to deflect some of the words' wounding power. I don't think I'm overstating this. When every word that describes you begins with a negative prefix, you begin to sense that you're not one of society's favorites. What I could never understand is why when a man leaves a woman with a baby, the woman is labeled the failure. Okay, now I'm getting cranky. Let's move on.

SOLO RULE #8:
Re: Other men.

I'm not talking about dating here. I'm talking about bringing a male influence into your child's life. Most books on single mothering encourage you to do this. It sounds like logical advice, but the implementation of it can feel awfully contrived and awkward. I had no brothers or male family nearby, so I kept trying to envision ways I could finagle my male friends into spending time with Lulu. Short of offering sexual favors and/or martinis, I wasn't coming up with many creative hooks, but the books said to do it, so I worried quite a bit that I wasn't making it happen. In time, quite naturally, several of my straight and gay male friends did end up spending lots of time over at my house. And they loved Lulu and she loved them. The point is, another person's love for your child is a gift, not a device you can activate. (And by the way, female love counts, too.)

SOLO RULE #9:
Stop feeling sorry for your little one.

I spent a lot of time in this cesspool and can still wade in there on days when my defenses are down. Having seen what

it has done to my stepkids, I can tell you without equivoca-
tion: You need to fight the temptation to consider your child
a victim. (Unless of course there is real abuse or neglect, and
then you need to take immediate legal and police action.) If
you didn't purposely plan to have a child alone—or even if
you did—it can be devastating to fully realize that your child
is not going to have a "normal" home with two parents loving
her to pieces and tucking her in bed every night. Far be it from
me to underplay that disappointment. But don't make your
child the victim you're afraid she will become. It's important
to remember that your child is incredibly lucky, too—to have
you. And there are so many worse things that could have happened—like you staying with the lying, cheating bonehead,
for instance. So by all means, work through your grief over
the death of that "intact household" dream, and stay compassionate and open to the difficulties your child will face. Then
trust that you will be able to give your child the resilience and
grace to make the most of the hand she was dealt. Leading by
example couldn't hurt.

SOLO RULE #10:
Get over yourself.
Okay, here's a harsh dose of reality . . . which is also oddly comforting. Nobody's that interested in you. It's not that you're
anything less than fascinating, darling. It's just the 99.8 Percent Rule. Here's how it works: At any given point in time,
96 percent of a person's attention is focused on his favorite

subject: Himself! Top that off with another 3.8 percent of attention that's devoted to spouse, kids, fantasy football, Pamela Anderson, climate change, and other global priorities. That leaves a whopping .2 percent of attention for everything else on the planet, including you. So when you're feeling horribly self-conscious out in public, thinking that everyone is sitting in harsh judgment of you, remember the 99.8 percent rule. And breathe a little easier. Why, you're practically *anonymous*!

SOLO RULE #11:
Avoid holidays if they torment you.

The best Thanksgiving I ever spent when Lulu was young was the Thanksgiving she and I spent by ourselves in the fabulous Miramar Hotel overlooking the beach in Santa Monica. We flew out of Denver about noon on Thursday, arrived in the deserted hotel about 4 P.M., and spent most of the dinner hour lying on our backs in the pool, looking up into the palm trees. We didn't see so much as a drumstick of turkey, slammed down some Scotch (me) and soda (Lulu) for dinner, and bounced as high as we could from bed to bed until we were exhausted. It was perfect. Yes, I was escaping reality—and it worked!

Now, I love family holidays, and I love my family. But sometimes the idea of celebrating a family holiday when you don't feel like you're a family—or at least not the family you envisioned being—is simply unbearable. Go with that feeling. I kept trying to fit in with friends who were nice enough to ask me over and make me feel welcome, but inside, I always felt like odd man out; the obligatory orphan at the table. I didn't want to go home, because all my siblings are happily married and totally nuclear. It was incredibly liberating to realize I didn't have to suffer through these holidays, which were making me miserable. I hereby give you permission to do the same. Until your child is old enough to really miss a holiday (and kids generally will never miss Thanksgiving), don't feel guilty about skipping it. In fact, it can be blissfully bohemian, unconventional, and empowering to simply decide that you get to choose the holidays you're going to celebrate. You're entitled. I said so.

SOLO RULE #12:
Spill the family secrets.

If your child is "illegitimate," you may decide that this information is so hurtful, you'd rather keep it a "secret." And so, you concoct the fable that you were married and got divorced, or Daddy was a Buddhist monk whose deep religious calling forced him to return to the monastery, or that Pop lost his life bravely serving in the SPCA. Okay. That's pretty creative. But I must forewarn you that no matter how good your story is, or how rigorous your policing of all information that might expose the truth, family secrets of any kind are very rarely successfully kept. For one thing, children just have an innate sense of the truth (which doesn't mean they won't all turn into pathological fibbers once they hit puberty—no, make that two years old). A family secret lies there like a bump under the rug, and even though everybody steps carefully around it and averts their eyes, sooner or later somebody is going to trip right over it and the whole stinking thing is going to get dragged out in the open. And the longer it's been lurking under wraps, the uglier it becomes when it's pulled out into the cold light of day.

Knowing what a blabbermouth I am, I suspected the odds that I was going to be able to pull off a lifetime deception

Get thee to a Bible

Maybe you're out of the habit, or maybe you never were in it. Whatever. Get yourself a Bible and when you're feeling awful, open it up and read a Psalm. (8, 18, 19, 23, 27, 33, 40, 46, 55, 62, 67, 72, 91, 95, 101, 103, 104, 121, and 128 are big favorites). When you're feeling sad, lonely, helpless, desperate, or scared, it's a powerful thing to imbibe. For one thing, the language is lush and gorgeous. For another, it's much bigger than you and your measly problems, which is always reassuring. And finally, almost everywhere you look, the Bible is saying "Fear not," and holding out help and hope. You don't have to be a Christian; you can stay right back there in the Old Testament if you want, and you don't have to wade through all those begats and beheadings. (If you haven't spent much time in Deuteronomy lately, you may have forgotten that the Good Book is packed with blood and gore.) You don't even have to believe. But don't deny yourself what is right at hand. Pick up the Book and put your hands together when you're feeling alone. It can really help.

were slim, indeed. I also didn't want to make the reality of being illegitimate seem shameful and scandalous, something you needed to cover up. And above all, I wanted to avoid that killer question, "So what else did you lie to me about?"

I was, basically, too scared to lie. What I discovered is that by telling Lulu the truth right from the start, I (hopefully) robbed the event of its drama and deflected its sting. She knows she was wanted, she knows she is loved, and she knows that some people will be shocked by the fact her parents weren't married. Instead of keeping her safe with a lie, I armed her with the truth. That's my story and I'm sticking to it.

SOLO RULE #13:
A very meaningful money disclaimer.

As I may have mentioned, I was supremely lucky to be financially secure when I became a single mother. I had worked for twenty-odd years, tucked away savings like the little Catholic squirrel I truly am, and had enough money in the bank to give me the liberty to make the choices I wanted. Not everyone is so fortunate. In no way do I want to gloss over this fact, or make light of the very real difficulties faced by millions of mothers who struggle daily to make ends meet. My emotional hardships seem . . . well, shallow . . . when compared to the trauma of not having enough food for your kids, or trying to find a decent place to live. To my mind, the single mothers who are trying to raise their children in dire financial circumstances are the real heroines of our world.

SOLO RULE #14:
Eat out loud.

Going out to public places with a baby can pose special challenges for a single mom. You may feel as if you're the object of people's contempt or pity. Or just a general pain in the rear, since many people do not, in fact, like children—particularly babies. First, reread Solo Rule #10: Get over yourself. Then realize that most people a) do not know that the baby's father ditched you, b) assume Daddy is on a business trip or playing golf, or c) don't really care one way or the other; they just want you to get that baby away from them. During my first month with Lulu, the one place I longed to go was to the movies. My first matinee went off without a hitch, and I felt adventurous and invisible in the darkened theater. My second attempt was on a Friday night and was thwarted when, after standing in a huge line, I was told quite loudly that babies were not permitted in the theater after six and we would not be allowed to enter. Everyone stared at me with open hostility, noticing my lack of a wedding ring, I'm sure, and looking for the welfare check I was probably trying to cash to pay for my ticket. It was completely humiliating, and the memory of that kept me from going out alone for months.

Once Lulu got older, I felt the same reluctance to eat out alone—until I decided to simply head for restaurants packed with kids and pretend my husband was an international airline pilot, off on a pan-Asian tour. The Macaroni Grill was nice, because you could get a huge glass of red wine while you were waiting, and they provided crayons so your child could draw on the paper tablecloth. (This can be a difficult habit to break at home.)

Denny's was another big favorite. When Lulu was three, we would always go before church on Sunday mornings. Because it was ridiculously early, the place was crammed with seniors lured in by the $2.99 Grand Slam special. They cooed with admiration at my gorgeous little girl, all decked out in her Sunday dresses—until the day when Lulu, watching a big platter of pancakes being delivered to a table nearby, yelled, "Hey, where are *my* f***ing pancakes?" She had never used that word before and has never (to my severely limited knowledge) used it again. Total silence fell over Denny's while I racked my brain for a word that rhymed with "f***ing." Ever fast on my feet, I replied loudly, "Oh honey, you're not getting *buckwheat* pancakes!" But those old codgers weren't buying it. We didn't dare show our cute faces at Denny's for a year afterward, although you'll be happy to know we still went to church every week—religiously.

SOLO RULE #15:
Be proud.

Every time I see one of those gargantuan NBA players or somebody like Steven Spielberg stand up at the podium and thank his single mom for raising him, I get all choked up. I guess it's just the adult acknowledgment by the grown child for all that has been given, and its true cost. But however distant that gratitude seems to be (and right now, given Lulu's preadolescent disgust with me, I can safely say it's in another galaxy), I continue to believe that the bond between a child and his or her single mother is truly special. As immensely difficult as the journey is, at the end, when your child flies off with strong wings and a kind heart (or even flipping you the bird), your satisfaction must surely be doubly sweet.

Being proud of myself as a single mother was hard for me, because deep in my heart I felt a great deal of shame that Mr. Wrong had taken flight and I was raising my darling daughter alone. It took years for me to understand that in giving my heart to Mr. Wrong, I had made one of the worst possible investments of my life, yet earned the greatest conceivable return. And where's the shame in that? When I look back on pictures of Lulu and me, I wonder why I couldn't see how beautiful and brave we were. Long ago, when it was just the two of us.

Stand tall. Be proud of your strength and your ability to thrive. Give thanks for all you are and all you have been given. Amen.

Index

About the Author

Born in Niagara Falls and raised in Wilmington, Delaware as one of eight children, BETTY LONDERGAN spent over twenty years as a writer and creative director in advertising, working in Denver, San Francisco, and Philadelphia. Previously a single mother, she is now married to Lawrence Schall, the president of Oglethorpe University in Atlanta. They have four children: three of his, one of hers, and a big, fat cat. This is her first book.